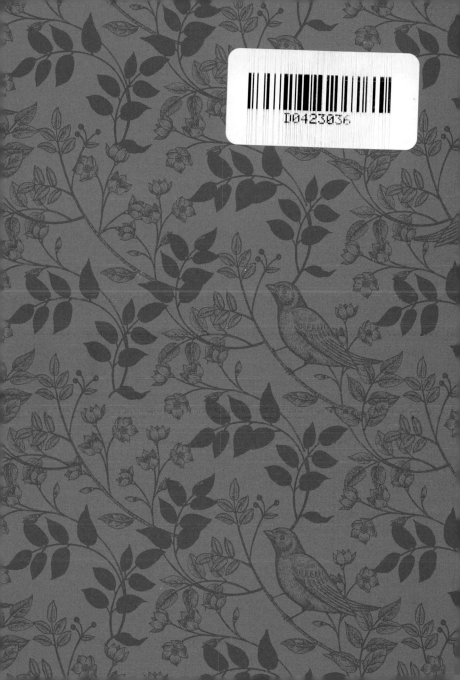

TO:

Mom

FROM:

Abby : Krystle

DATE:

Christmas 2020

Published by Christian Art Publishers
PO Box 1599, Vereeniging, 1930, RSA

© 2018
First edition 2018

Designed by Christian Art Publishers

Images used under license from Shutterstock.com

Printed in China

ISBN 978-14321-2839-5

18 19 20 21 22 23 24 25 26 27 – 10 9 8 7 6 5 4 3 2 1

WHO IS THE HOLY *Spirit?*

EXPERIENCING GOD'S POWER

Nancy Taylor
& Philip Ryken

CHRISTIAN ART PUBLISHERS

Contents

The Holy Spirit in the life of individuals

How we relate to the Holy Spirit

The gifts of the Spirit

INTRODUCTION

This book was my sister Nancy's idea. As a mother of five, she hears lots of questions every day. In my role as the President of Wheaton College I hear lots of questions too, including theological questions.

The most important questions that anyone can ask are about God and how we relate to Him: *Who is God? Why did Jesus die on the cross? What does it mean to be a Christian?*

The answers to these questions help us understand the meaning of our existence and open the door to eternal life. But they are only the beginning. Once we enter into a personal friendship with God, we want to learn as much about Him as we can, and one of the best ways to learn is by asking more questions. In this book we turn to the third Person of the Trinity, the Holy Spirit: *Who is the Holy Spirit? What is His role in the life of a believer? How can the Spirit help me be more like Jesus?*

We hope that this book will help give some answers. We wrote it mainly for people who are new to Christianity, but it is really for anyone who is curious about God and wants to know Him better.

There are sixty questions in all – just the right number for reading one question (and one answer) every day for two months. We have tried to put plenty of Scripture into our answers – partly because the Bible is the only place to get reliable information about God, and partly because we hope that some people will use this book for their daily devotions.

Nancy did most of the writing, and I did most of the editing. So I suppose our relationship is typical: the younger sibling does most of the work, while the older sibling makes the corrections and takes half the credit.

But we wrote this book for you. And our prayer for you is simply this: that the Holy Spirit will help you to know Jesus' love in a deeper way, and that you will be filled to overflowing with the Holy Spirit's power and presence in your life.

~ Philip Ryken

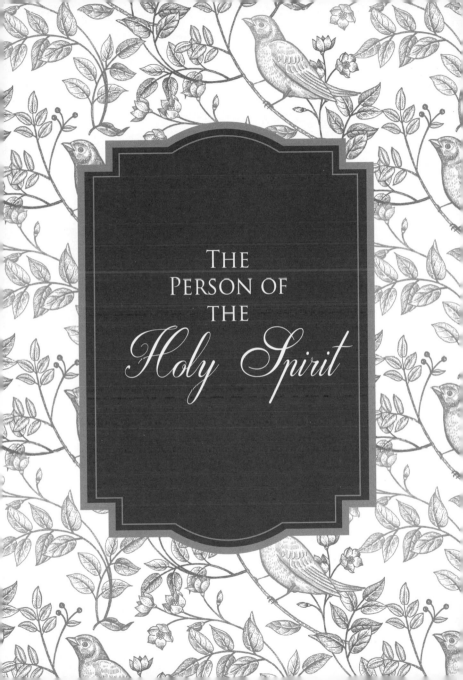

THE
PERSON OF
THE
Holy Spirit

1

Is the Holy Spirit a person?

There is a great deal of mystery surrounding the third person of the Trinity – the Holy Spirit. Most of us aren't quite sure what to think of Him ... or is that even the proper pronoun for the Holy Spirit? Should we say *Him* or *It*? Let's start there.

Throughout Scripture, the Holy Spirit is portrayed as equal in divinity and personality to God the Father and God the Son. Matthew 28:19 commands us to "Go therefore and make disciples of all nations, baptizing them in the name of the Father and of the Son and of the Holy Spirit." Similarly, the apostle Paul blessed the Corinthians with these words: "The grace of the Lord Jesus Christ and the love of God and the fellowship of the Holy Spirit be with you all" (2 Cor. 13:14). There is no hierarchy noted here, simply one God in Three Persons, with the Holy Spirit being as much a personal God as the loving Father and the gracious Son.

Furthermore, the Holy Spirit is personal in His dealings with us.

He leads and directs us (Acts 15:28; 16:6-7). He has a mind (Rom. 8:27) and a will (1 Cor. 12:11). He has emotions such as love (Gal. 5:22) and grief (Eph. 4:30). He acts – searching (1 Cor. 2:10), speaking (Rev. 2:7), interceding (Rom. 8:26), testifying (Jn. 15:26), teaching (Jn. 16:13; Neh. 9:20), and comforting (Jn. 14:16). Perhaps most telling of all, the Holy Spirit is affected by our actions and attitudes (Acts 5:3; Mt. 12:31-32; Heb. 10:29). Surely that is evidence enough that the Holy Spirit is, indeed, a person – a *He*, not an *It* (even if, strictly speaking, the Spirit does not have a gender).

Nevertheless, there is more mystery surrounding the person of the Holy Spirit than there is about God the Father or God the Son. We understand the Father-Son relationship from our own experience. Because of our humanity, we can also grasp something of how God became a man, and maybe even the bodily sacrifice He made before the Father on our behalf. But the Holy Spirit's person and work isn't quite as clear-cut. The Spirit is wind and breath that blows where It pleases (Jn. 3:8). The Spirit rarely calls attention to Himself, for He exists to glorify the Son and the Father. And we can't predict how or where the Holy Spirit will act, but only know after the fact that He has come.

> *"Go therefore and make disciples of all nations, baptizing them in the name of the Father and of the Son and of the Holy Spirit."*
>
> MATTHEW 28:19

For these reasons, we sometimes miss the Spirit's presence and may be tempted to ignore His work. But we had better not ignore Him, for the Holy Spirit is the means by which the salvation of Jesus Christ is applied to our lives. He is essential for salvation and sanctification and resurrection life. As we study the Spirit, let's see if we can unveil some of the mystery, coming to a fuller understanding of the Holy Spirit's ways so we can take deeper hold of the full beauty of God's work in the world.

2

Is God the Holy Spirit equal with God the Father and God the Son?

The Christian faith depends on the interworking of the Three Persons of the Godhead, what we often call the Trinity: God the Father, God the Son, and God the Holy Spirit. If you take away any one of these Persons, you no longer have true, Biblical Christianity. But because of the Holy Spirit's role – His willing subordination to and glorification of Christ and the mysterious, sometimes hidden nature of His work – it is sometimes easy to think of the Holy Spirit as less divine than the Father and the Son. Indeed, this is an erroneous teaching that has plagued the church throughout history, beginning with Arius (A.D. 250–336) and continuing down through modern-day Mormons and Jehovah's Witnesses. So let's explore what the Bible teaches about the Spirit.

The Holy Spirit has the same divine attributes as the Father and the Son. He is holy (Rom. 1:4), eternal (Heb. 9:14), and omnipresent (Ps. 139:7). He is omnipotent, able to do all things by His mighty power (Lk. 1:35; Zec. 4:6). He is all-knowing (1 Cor. 2:10-11; Isa. 40:13). These are attributes that can only belong to God – and are in fact the attributes that make God to be God – so the fact that the Holy Spirit is described in these terms proves His full divinity. He is just as divine as the Father and Son are.

The Holy Spirit also acts in ways that only God can act. He creates out of nothing (Gen. 1:2; Job 33:4). He regenerates, bringing *spiritual* life – something that by definition only the Holy Spirit can bring about – where there was previously death (Jn. 3:5, 7). He inspired holy Scripture and is thus the author of truth (2 Pet. 1:20-21). And He is the one who will give us eternal resurrection life (Rom. 8:11). So although He takes a more hidden role in the saving works of God, all of the Holy Spirit's works are activities that belong to God alone, and therefore He is equal to the Father and the Son.

We will unpack the implications of this truth throughout this book, answering questions about the Holy Spirit's work in God's saving plan, revealing what the Holy Spirit means in a believer's daily life, and showing how we should respond to the Spirit's work. Hopefully, by the end of this study the Holy Spirit will be a bit less mysterious. As you come to understand how pervasive and how life-changing the Holy Spirit's indwelling presence is, He will begin to play a larger role in your spiritual walk, and you will be able to more deeply experience God's love for you.

---

*The Spirit of God has made me, and the
breath of the Almighty gives me life.*

JOB 33:4

3

If the Holy Spirit is equally God, why does He glorify the Son?

Human nature bristles at being in a position of subservience. We want to be in charge of our own lives, and perhaps the lives of others as well. We long for self-actualization, if not self-glorification. The idea that anyone would willingly spend their entire existence bringing honor and glory to another is almost unthinkable. Yet this is the role that the Holy Spirit willingly and joyfully takes.

As we have seen, the Spirit is fully equal to the Son. Yet Jesus described the Holy Spirit's work like this: "He will glorify me, for he will take what is mine and declare it to you" (Jn. 16:14). In other words, the Holy Spirit dedicates Himself to glorifying Jesus Christ, helping us understand our Savior's teaching, pointing to His saving work on the cross, and promising His return in glory. The Spirit takes Christ's love and shows it to us, declaring it vividly at times, and whispering it at others. His message is not His own; He lives to draw attention to Another.

We often think about the great humility Jesus displayed on our behalf, the immortal taking on the mortal and then suffering and dying to save us. This is the mystery of the Incarnation, of God with us. Yet the Holy Spirit displays humility as well, for He condescends to dwell with us and in us permanently, living in our sin-ridden hearts to point us not to Himself, but to Another – Jesus the risen Christ. This is an omnipresent expression of love, a continual gift of grace for our good and Christ's glory.

It is important to note that being fully God, the Holy Spirit could do anything He wants to do. The role He takes in applying the work of God the Father and God the Son to us is a role He willingly takes for our redemption. Herein lies a challenge for us. Our lives also should be centered on glorifying Christ – not on ourselves, or even on a particular theology, but on Jesus Christ. As the Westminster Shorter Catechism summarizes for us, our "chief end is to glorify God, and to enjoy Him forever." If we want to be in accord with the Holy Spirit, we must set ourselves to the task of making much of Christ – of taking His love and declaring it to others.

"The Helper, the Holy Spirit, whom the Father will send in my name, he will teach you all things and bring to your remembrance all that I have said to you."

JOHN 14:26

The truth that the Holy Spirit points to Christ also serves as an important litmus test for the church. Anything that focuses too much on the Person of the Holy Spirit is not of the Spirit, for He points to Christ. And anything that adds to the message of Scripture is also not of the Spirit, for He declares the message of Christ, which is fully disclosed in Scripture. We must subject any teaching about the Holy Spirit or words from the Holy Spirit to this test: Does it point to Christ? And does it draw to mind the message of Christ, the gospel?

THE
Holy Spirit
AND JESUS

4

What was the Holy Spirit's role in the virgin birth?

The Holy Spirit's work of glorifying the Son of God and applying salvation to us began in earnest at the moment of Jesus' Incarnation, the moment He was conceived in the womb of a young virgin named Mary. The story begins in Luke 1:30, when the angel Gabriel came to Mary and told her that she was a recipient of God's grace – His undeserved favor. This grace would have a specific manifestation: Mary would bear a son, and He would be the Son of the Most High, taking the forever throne of His ancestor David.

The startling revelation of an angel, bringing an even more startling revelation of God's work in her life, no doubt brought to mind many questions for young Mary. But she was immediately submissive to God's messenger, and so she just asked one humble question, a question born not of doubt but of curiosity: "How will this be, since I am a virgin?" (v. 34).

Mary's virginity was important for two reasons. It meant that as an unmarried woman she was sexually pure, and it meant she couldn't be pregnant already. In other words, there would be no mistaking that her child was the supernatural work of God. In human terms, what the angel promised was an impossibility (v. 37).

This is where the Holy Spirit enters the story. How would this miraculous manifestation of God's grace be applied to Mary? Through the Holy Spirit. How is grace always applied to human beings, each time there is a miraculous work of God? Through the Holy Spirit. As the angel said to Mary, "The Holy Spirit will come upon you, and the power of the Most High will overshadow you; therefore the child to be born will be called holy – the Son of God" (v. 35).

The Holy Spirit will come upon you, and the power of the Most High will overshadow you; therefore the child to be born will be called holy – the Son of God … For nothing will be impossible with God.

LUKE 1:35, 37

The details of how this would happen are not given, but the mechanism is clear. The Holy Spirit would act, and therefore a virgin would conceive. The Holy Spirit would act, and therefore this child would be the divine Son of God.

The greatest mystery of all time – the fullness of God in human flesh (Col. 2:9) – would occur through the quiet mystery of the Holy Spirit's ministry. The so-called "shy" member of the Trinity was given the task of quietly incarnating the Christ as the Savior of the world. This miraculous conception is an impossible work that only God Himself could orchestrate, the Holy Spirit implanting the seed of God the Son's salvation by the will of God the Father.

Beyond the wonder of the Incarnation, there is a lesson here for us about the Holy Spirit's work today. This same quiet overshadowing of people and circumstances is how the Holy Spirit often imparts God's grace to us. He draws attention not to Himself, but to Jesus. He acts to apply salvation to us, orchestrating and ordering events to bring us to the cross and the empty tomb so that we can bow our hearts and our lives before the Most High God. This, too, is a mystery, an impossible miracle.

5

What was the Holy Spirit's role in the baptism of Jesus?

Jesus' public ministry began with the notable event of His baptism by John. Each of the Gospels records this signal event in the life of Jesus, and each one describes the Holy Spirit descending like a dove on Jesus at the same moment God the Father expresses His approval of Him with the words "you are my beloved Son; with you I am well pleased" (Mk. 1:11; Lk. 3:22).

It is important to note first of all what the Holy Spirit's descent on Jesus at His baptism is not. This was not the beginning of the Spirit's work in Jesus' life. As we have already seen, the Holy Spirit initiated the Savior's conception. In addition, we know that Jesus was endowed with Spirit-given wisdom as a child (Lk. 2:40). Jesus was already indwelt with the Spirit and filled with the Spirit prior to His baptism. So what was God's purpose in rending heaven for the descent of the Spirit on Jesus?

The descent of the Holy Spirit at Jesus' baptism initiated a new phase in Jesus' life and ministry. He was being anointed and empowered for a particular task, the time when He would usher in the Messianic age and baptize others with the Holy Spirit (Jn. 1:33). This anointing is similar to the way the Spirit came upon prophets in the Old Testament at their commissioning. Jesus needed this special Holy Spirit anointing to be equipped for the rigors that lay before Him: His temptation in the wilderness, the challenges of His earthly ministry, and the suffering of the cross. He was being anointed for battle so He could take on the powers of darkness and overcome them.

The baptism of Jesus was also a tangible reminder to Jesus of His Father's love and a proof of His identity as the Messiah. At the moment when His work would begin in earnest, Jesus received a public testimony of His role as the Son of God. The Holy Spirit was acting as the agent of prophetic endowment, descending as a seal of the Father's approval.

All Three Persons of the Godhead were present to confirm the deity of Christ; the voice of God and the Spirit of God reinforced the Messianic role of Jesus as the Son of God.

The same Holy Spirit who descended on Jesus at His baptism also descends on us. The Spirit is not usually visible to others, and true to His nature, His work may be almost hidden to us as well, but the Spirit empowers us for spiritual battles and new phases of ministry. He gives us special moments when we sense the Father's love. He leads us into spiritual battle, just as He led Jesus into the wilderness to be tempted. And He gives us the power we need to do the will of God.

And when Jesus was baptized, immediately he went up from the water, and behold, the heavens were opened to him, and he saw the Spirit of God descending like a dove and coming to rest on him; and behold, a voice from heaven said, "This is my beloved Son, with whom I am well pleased."

MATTHEW 3:16-17

6

What was the Holy Spirit's role in the earthly ministry of Jesus?

Everywhere Jesus went, people marveled at the authority with which He spoke and the marvels He performed. Since Jesus is God, we might assume that His teaching and healing ministry rested on His own power. But this would be a wrong assumption; Scripture tells us that in all aspects of His ministry, the source of Jesus' power was the Holy Spirit. In the mystery of the Trinity, Jesus the Son of God did the works of God the Father through the power of God the Holy Spirit.

When the Pharisees accused Jesus of working under the power of Satan to cast out demons, Jesus told them, "it is by the Spirit of God that I cast out demons" (Mt. 12:28). Just a few verses before, Matthew quoted the prophet Isaiah, saying, "I will put my Spirit upon him, and he will proclaim justice to the Gentiles" (Mt. 12:18). Later on, Peter would also draw a clear connection between Jesus' ministry and the power of the Holy Spirit. He preached, "God anointed Jesus of Nazareth with the Holy Spirit and with power. He went about doing good and healing all who were oppressed by the devil, for God was with him" (Acts 10:38). The witness of the prophets, of Jesus Himself, and of the disciples all attribute the power of Jesus to the indwelling Holy Spirit.

This would all be a historical fact with little impact on the daily life of the believer, if it weren't for an astonishing statement from the lips of Jesus. In His farewell discourse to the disciples, Jesus said, "Truly, truly, I say to you, whoever believes in me will also do the works that I do; and *greater works* than these will he do, because I am going to the Father" (Jn. 14:12, emphasis added). How could anyone possibly do greater works than Jesus Himself? The following verses provide the answer when they talk about the coming of the Holy Spirit. In short, Jesus said that through the power of the Holy Spirit, believers today can do even greater works than He did while He was on earth.

The coming of the Holy Spirit to indwell believers – something

"Truly, truly, I say to you, whoever believes in me will also do the works that I do; and greater works than these will he do, because I am going to the Father."

JOHN 14:12

that was only possible because Jesus returned to Heaven to facilitate His coming – enables us to extend the reach of God's power throughout the earth. No longer is the work of Jesus limited to Galilee or even to Judea, but it extends to every nation, tribe, and language on the earth. Whereas the incarnate Christ could only be in one place at one time, the Holy Spirit goes with believers wherever we go to share the gospel. This is what Jesus meant by "greater works." As God's people pray in His name and minister in reliance on the Holy Spirit, we can be instruments of God's healing in the hearts and lives of people all over the world. We get to participate in the ministry of Jesus – doing good and healing those who are oppressed – using the same tool He used: the power of the Holy Spirit who lives inside us.

7

What was the Holy Spirit's role in the crucifixion and resurrection of Jesus?

If the Spirit was the source of Jesus' power when He performed miracles and preached the good news of salvation, was He also involved in the central event of Jesus' mission – His death and resurrection? The Bible tells us that He was. The Holy Spirit who hovered over the moment of conception and walked with Jesus through each day of His earthly life was with Him at the moment He yielded His spirit to death and then raised Him in power from the grave.

The writer of Hebrews makes explicit the relationship between the Spirit and Jesus' death: "How much more will the blood of Christ, *who through the eternal Spirit* offered himself without blemish to God, purify our conscience from dead works to serve the living God" (Heb. 9:14, emphasis added). Jesus relied on the Holy Spirit for comfort and strength to endure the suffering and shame of the cross. Perhaps He could have done it without the Spirit's help, but He chose not to. The good news for us is that the same Spirit who empowered Jesus to face suffering and death also comforts us in our weakness, soothing our souls with words of truth and applying to our hearts the reassuring promises of God (Jn. 14:26).

The Holy Spirit is also the source of resurrection life. The apostle Paul makes this connection clear: "If the Spirit of him who raised Jesus from the dead dwells in you, he who raised Christ Jesus from the dead will also give life to your mortal bodies through his Spirit who dwells in you" (Rom. 8:11). Resurrection power comes through the Holy Spirit, and this is true for us just as it was for Jesus. The same Spirit that raised Jesus from the dead will also raise us from the dead.

> *If the Spirit of him who raised Jesus from the dead dwells in you, he who raised Christ Jesus from the dead will also give life to your mortal bodies through his Spirit who dwells in you.*
>
> ROMANS 8:11

Like the Spirit, the Father and the Son were intimately involved in the death and resurrection of Christ. In the infinite wisdom of God, all three members of the Trinity – Father, Son, and Holy Spirit – were integrally involved in all aspects of salvation. They filled different roles and performed different tasks, but all were at work in the process that brings us life.

The important thing to note in these verses is that Jesus' work in and through the Spirit was *for us*. Jesus' death is what enables us to bury our dead works so we can serve the living God. And the Spirit's resurrection power will one day give life to our mortal bodies, raising us up to dwell with Christ. In this life and the next, true life is only available to us through the Holy Spirit. He is the One who unites us with Christ in His death so that we can rise to new life in Christ (Rom. 6:4-5).

8

What was the Holy Spirit's role in the ascension and glorification of Jesus?

The journey of Jesus was completed in His return to the Father in glory. Jesus was not just raised from the dead; He was also seated with God in the heavenly places as proof of the sufficiency of the atonement He made for sinners and the victory He won over the grave (Eph. 1:20-23). In heaven He took His rightful place as King and Judge. Here, too, in this climactic act of Jesus' salvation work, the Holy Spirit is present as the One who glorifies God the Son.

Jesus' ascension is important to us because it enabled the Holy Spirit to be present with His people (Jn. 14-16). As Jesus told the disciples, if He did not return to the Father, the Holy Spirit would not come to us (Jn. 16:7). The Holy Spirit's presence and power in our lives is only possible because of the ascension of the risen Lord Jesus Christ. So you could say that the Holy Spirit's role after the ascension of Jesus was to descend to us and finish the work of glorifying Jesus in our lives.

The Spirit's aim is to glorify Christ, and one of the primary ways He does this is by applying to us the gift of salvation. We are vessels for the Spirit's glorification of the Son of God as He recreates us in the image of Christ. The Spirit shares with us the presence and power of the enthroned Christ, thereby making Christ visible in us. As we are filled with the glorious Spirit, we can live to glorify Christ. Indeed, our chief end or primary purpose, as the Westminster Shorter Catechism tells us, is to "glorify God and enjoy him forever".

Our citizenship is in heaven, and from it we await a Savior, the Lord Jesus Christ, who will transform our lowly body to be like his glorious body, by the power that enables him even to subject all things to himself.

PHILIPPIANS 3:20-21

The Holy Spirit enables us to glorify Christ by applying salvation to us and teaching us what Christ has done. We participate in the task of growing in obedience so that our lives bring greater honor and fuller glory to our Savior. We should ask ourselves, *In my life goals and daily interactions, is Jesus glorified? In my leisure pursuits and time management, is Jesus glorified?* And perhaps most importantly, *Am I relying on the Holy Spirit's indwelling power, allowing Him to teach me and change me?*

The Holy Spirit's glorification of Jesus in the lives of believers is for the here-and-now as we grow to increasingly reflect the character of the risen Christ. It is also a future event. One day we will be raised glorious in Christ to eternal life, sharing in His inheritance and enjoying citizenship in our heavenly home.

This future glorification of those who are saved by the blood of Jesus includes moral perfection (Heb. 2:10-11) and a glorious resurrection body (Phil. 3:21), similar to the glorious body that the Spirit gave the Son when He raised Him from the dead. This promise is our certain hope – what we live for.

29

9

Why did Jesus have to leave in order for the Holy Spirit to come?

It sure would be nice to be able to see Jesus face-to-face and ask Him all our questions. Even better would be if He had set up an earthly kingdom after His resurrection, like the disciples expected Him to. But would this truly be better? Jesus tells us that it wouldn't. In fact, He told the disciples that it was *better* for Him to leave. He said, "It is to your advantage that I go away, for if I do not go away, the Helper will not come to you. But if I go, I will send him to you" (Jn. 16:7). In other words, the Holy Spirit would not come unless Jesus left, and the Holy Spirit's work was so important that having Him is better than having Jesus stay on earth! This leaves us with two questions: why did Jesus have to leave in order for the Spirit to come, and how is it better to have the Spirit with us than to have Jesus stay on earth?

Jesus' earthly ministry was focused on one main event – His death for our sins, plus His subsequent resurrection. His role in our redemption was a one-time event, and when He had been raised from the dead that part of our salvation was complete. His ascension marks the end of that era in salvation history. But there is an ongoing aspect of salvation as well, whereby the message of salvation is carried to the ends of the earth and applied to the hearts of individual people.

This internal transformation that comes through the gift of new birth, conviction of sin, and growth in righteousness is the Holy Spirit's work. Jesus Christ, the incarnate Son of God confined to the limitations of humanity, could not do this internal work. Only the infinite, invisible Spirit can do this. And in God's wisdom, these two eras in salvation history could not coexist. It was only when Jesus' work was finished – signified by His return to heaven – that the Spirit's true work could begin, for He takes Jesus' death and resurrection and applies it to our minds and hearts.

This brings us to our second question: How is it better to have the Spirit with us than to have Jesus present in His earthly body? The answer lies in the different roles of each member of the Godhead. Jesus worked salvation for the whole world, whereas the Spirit works it into the heart of each individual believer.

In His physical body, Jesus was limited to one place at a time, whereas the Spirit simultaneously dwells in the heart of every believer in the entire world. Jesus' ministry was a once-for-all event, whereas the Spirit's ministry is a daily, minute-by-minute, ongoing and continuous event.

"Nevertheless, I tell you the truth: it is to your advantage that I go away, for if I do not go away, the Helper will not come to you. But if I go, I will send him to you."

John 16:7

The Spirit's mysterious indwelling is what enables us to be convicted, comforted, and empowered. He is able to help each believer simultaneously in an intimate and personalized way. And He is able to help us from the inside out. So what Jesus said is true: His departure and His sending of the Spirit are an advantage for us every day!

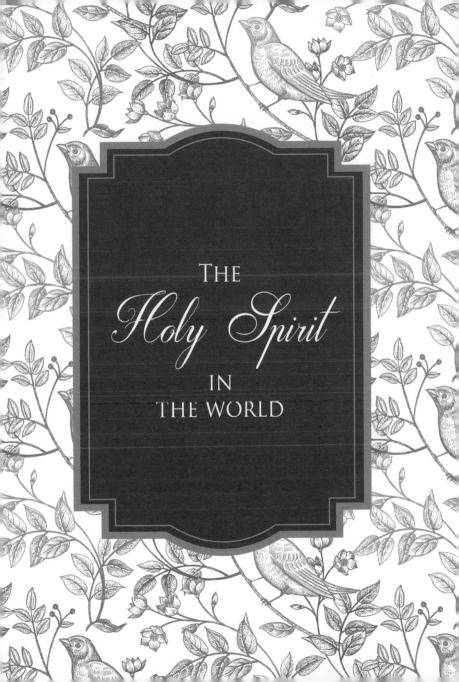

THE
Holy Spirit
IN
THE WORLD

10

What was the Spirit's role in revelation?

Christians center their lives around one book – *The Book* – the Bible. We do so because the Bible contains the words of God to us. By its writings we are able to understand who God is, who we are, and what God wants from us. In its pages we find His commands for how we should live today and His plan of salvation that enables us to have true life forever.

First, a brief history lesson. The Bible contains 66 books, written over a span of about 1300 years in various parts of the Middle East, North Africa, Europe, and Central Asia. There are over 40 authors represented in its pages, from a wide range of social and cultural backgrounds. It contains a vast array of literary genres, from legal documents to poetry and everything in between. Various parts were originally written in Hebrew, Greek, and Aramaic. This is a diverse book!

And yet, it is amazingly unified. Every page of

the Bible points to one person, the Messiah, who would come to rescue humanity from the curse of sin and death that we had brought on ourselves from the opening days of the earth. The picture of God that the Bible presents is amazingly consistent, too. He is the all-powerful Creator, holy and just but also infinitely merciful and loving. How could this collection of books from so many different people and time periods and cultures be so consistent in its message? The answer is that the entire Bible came through the mind of a single Author: the Holy Spirit.

Peter tells us that the Bible was written not by the will of man, but by the will of God (2 Pet. 1:21). Every word was breathed out by the Spirit into the hearts and minds of the prophets, apostles, poets, and historians God used to produce this Book of books (2 Tim. 3:16-17). It is because of the Holy Spirit's indwelling and empowering presence with them as they wrote that the Word of God came to be. That is not to say that the Bible does not contain the creativity and individuality of its various authors – the Spirit used the experiences and "quickened" the talents that God had in His sovereignty provided for them. But the entire process and the end result is divinely inspired through the work of the Spirit, and therefore the Bible is the complete communication of God to His people with no errors or omissions. We can know God through the Scriptures of the Old and New Testaments because the Spirit ensured that they are God's Word to us, His living and active Word that penetrates our souls and judges our hearts (Heb. 4:12).

As we daily turn to the words of God in Holy Scripture, we have the distinct advantage of having the Author living inside us to illuminate these words of truth (1 Cor. 2:10-12). The same Spirit who wrote God's Word teaches us and helps us to understand in our minds and with our hearts the message of God. What a wonder it is to have the Spirit's supernatural help as we read and study the Bible!

For no prophecy was ever produced by the will of man, but men spoke from God as they were carried along by the Holy Spirit.

2 Peter 1:21

11

What was the Spirit's role in creation?

We usually think of God the Father as the Creator of all things, and indeed He is. When the Scripture says, "In the beginning, God created the heavens and the earth," the simple word "God" makes us think of our heavenly Father (Gen. 1:1).

Perhaps we also think of Jesus as Creator, citing John 1:3: "All things were made through him, and without him was not any thing made that was made." But did you know that the Holy Spirit is also the Creator? Right after saying that God created the heavens and the earth, Genesis 1:2 states that "the Spirit of God was hovering over the face of the waters." At the moment of creation, when God called into being everything that is, all three members of the Trinity were present and active. God the Father spoke a word, Jesus acted as the agent of creation, and the Holy Spirit was brooding over the entire process. The Father spoke, the Son and the Spirit responded, and there was.

The word for *Spirit* is the same as the word for *breath*, and this opens up another layer of the Spirit's work in creation. The Holy

Spirit is especially involved in the creation of human life. The Genesis account tells us, "the LORD God formed the man of dust from the ground and breathed into his nostrils the breath of life, and the man became a living creature" (Gen. 2:7). Or consider Job 33:4, which uses the Spirit of God and the breath of life as poetic parallels: "The Spirit of God has made me, and the breath of the Almighty gives me life." The Holy Spirit is the breath of human life.

> *By the word of the LORD the heavens were made, and by the breath of his mouth all their host.*
>
> PSALM 33:6

The Spirit is also the sustainer of creation. Psalm 104 describes God's glorious creation, then points out that if the Spirit of God is withheld, things begin to wither and die. Verse 30 says, "When you send forth your Spirit, they are created, and you renew the face of the ground." It is the Spirit who gives life, and apart from Him there is no life at all. This also means that when we praise and glorify God for the beauty and splendor of creation, or for the way He provides for us each day, we should also praise the Spirit for these things.

These connections between creation and the work of the Spirit parallel an important truth about the role of the Holy Spirit in our lives. The Spirit moves and acts and works out the will of God. He is the active power who executes the thoughts of God. Or to put it another way, apart from the Spirit, God's will is not worked into the world or into the hearts of human beings. This means that apart from the Spirit we cannot have any part of the true life of salvation. Without the Spirit applying to our minds and hearts the work of Jesus at the cross, we remain dead in sin and destined for eternal death. He truly is our life, both in creation and in redemption.

12

Where was the Holy Spirit during the Old Testament?

We've seen how the Holy Spirit worked at Creation and in the earthly ministry of Jesus, and we know that He came to dwell permanently in the hearts of believers after Jesus' ascension. But where was He the rest of the time, throughout Old Testament history? Did He do anything then?

The Holy Spirit did not indwell every believer before the ascension of Christ, like He does now, but He was certainly present and active, working out God's purposes on the earth. References to the Spirit in the Old Testament speak of Him empowering people with knowledge, skill, and strength.

Those empowered by the Spirit with knowledge or wisdom include Moses and the seventy elders (Num. 11:17, 25) and Joshua (Num. 27:18; Dt. 34:9). God preserved and cared for His people by endowing their leaders with special wisdom to lead well, and this was done through a dispensation of the Holy Spirit. The Spirit was with them in a way that He was not with other people, and this gift was for the purpose of building up the nation of Israel, through whom God would bring salvation to the world.

The Spirit gave artistic and architectural skill to Bezalel to build the temple (Ex. 31:3; 35:31) and others to craft Aaron's priestly garments (Ex. 28:3). It can be said that any work done with excellence is in a general sense a gift of the Spirit, but these people were specially anointed by the Spirit to perform a particular task related to worship. Even in the Old Testament, God wanted to be worshiped in spirit and in truth, and with beauty that befits His holiness (Jn. 4:24).

"I am with you," declares the LORD of hosts, "according to the covenant that I made with you when you came out of Egypt. My Spirit remains in your midst. Fear not."

HAGGAI 2:4-5

The most common work of the Spirit in the Old Testament was to give strength and courage to particular men for the purpose of saving His people. Many of the judges received the Holy Spirit – most notably Samson, Othniel, Gideon, and Jephthah.

Also mentioned as having Spirit-endowed courage are Saul (1 Sam. 11:6) and David (1 Sam. 16:13). God raised up these men to fight for the welfare of His people, and He gave them special bravery to withstand the perils of war.

These workings of the Spirit in the Old Testament are similar to the things we see Him doing now, in our own lives. We rely on the Spirit to give us wisdom for how to live. He enlightens and empowers our natural abilities so that we can do everything to the glory of God. And He offers strength and courage in our inner being so that we can fend off Satan's attacks and face trials with hope. But we have an advantage over Old Testament believers, because the Spirit dwells in our hearts to give us all these things more continually and more permanently, from the moment of salvation until the moment we go to see Jesus face-to-face.

13

What happened at Pentecost?

Just as a gust of wind can blow a tiny spark into a great forest fire, so also the Holy Spirit's coming at Pentecost with the sound of wind and tongues of fire ignited the disciples' tiny spark of faith into a worldwide gospel movement. Pentecost was an exceptional event that had not happened before and has not happened in the same way since. It was the visible and audible sign that God had come to dwell in His people to convict them of sin and seal the salvation work that Jesus had done on the cross. It was a bold proclamation that Satan had been judged and his spell was broken.

This special pouring out of the Spirit on God's people was predicted by the prophet Joel many centuries before: "I will pour out my Spirit on all flesh; your sons and your daughters shall prophesy, your old men shall dream dreams, and your young men shall see visions" (Joel 2:28). Jesus also promised this supernatural and world-changing event: "Behold, I am sending the promise of my Father upon you. But stay in the city until you are clothed with power from on high" (Lk. 24:49).

In the second chapter of Acts these promises came true. Fifty days after Jesus had ascended, as the apostles waited in a room for the power Jesus had promised, "suddenly there came from heaven a sound like a mighty rushing wind, and it filled the entire house where they were sitting. And divided tongues as of fire appeared to them and rested on each one of them. And they were all filled with the Holy Spirit and began to speak in other tongues as the Spirit gave them utterance" (Acts 2:2-4).

This dramatic event was an undeniable visitation from God. The symbols accompanying Pentecost reveal the meaning behind it. Wind is traditionally a symbol of divinity – think of the dry bones in Ezekiel that received the breath of life (Ezek. 37) or the whirlwind from which God spoke to Job (Job 38:1). Wind symbolizes the presence of the mighty, energizing power of God. It also brings to mind the unpredictable and uncontrollable force of the Holy Spirit, as Jesus described to Nicodemus when he said, "The wind blows where it wishes, and you hear its sound, but you do not know where it comes from or where it goes. So it is with everyone who is born of the Spirit" (Jn. 3:8). Fire is also a sign of divinity – think of Moses and the burning bush or Solomon at the dedication of the Temple (Ex. 3; 2 Chr. 7:1; Heb. 12:29). Fire shows how God's presence illuminates, purifies, and inspires us.

Suddenly there came from heaven a sound like a mighty rushing wind, and it filled the entire house where they were sitting.

ACTS 2:2

Given the symbolism throughout Scripture of wind and fire, it is no surprise that the Holy Spirit's coming was accompanied by these signs. He is a powerful force that summons our zeal for the worship and service of God. He comes in great power in a way we can feel and brings forth spiritual fruit in our lives. The presence of the Spirit is the living proof that God has truly given us new life in Jesus.

What is the Holy Spirit's role in world events?

We know that the Spirit is active in the lives of Christians, but what about world events? Does the Holy Spirit have a role in what is going on in the world, or only in the hearts of believers? The Bible doesn't explicitly answer this question. The answer is one of inference and extrapolation, as is perhaps befitting for the "hidden" member of the Trinity.

It is important to note that the Holy Spirit only indwells believers. Throughout the New Testament there is a distinction made between those who have placed their trust in Jesus and those who have not.

Those who have not repented of their sin and received forgiveness through Jesus' death on the cross do not have the Spirit living inside them. But the moment we turn to Jesus in faith, acknowledging the ways we have fallen short of His perfect standard and trusting His death in our place, the Spirit comes and lives within us. We become a new creature, a temple of the Holy Spirit (Rom. 8:9; 1 Cor. 3:16). From that moment on, we are the beneficiaries of the Spirit's work as He reminds us of the truth and empowers us to walk in it.

Understanding the Spirit's work among those who do not trust in Jesus begins with the doctrine of common grace. This doctrine teaches that because every good and perfect gift is from God (James 1:17) and God is merciful to all His creatures (Mt. 5:45), all truth and beauty come from God, wherever they are found. If all truth is God's truth, and if the Holy Spirit is the member of the Trinity who acts out or energizes the purposes of God, then all the acts of God and all the ways He is at work in the world are in some way works of the Spirit. Therefore, the Holy Spirit is at work in raising up leaders (Rom. 13:1) and also in their downfall (Dan. 2:21). Through this and other means, He works to restrain evil in the world (Gen. 6:3; 2 Pet. 3:3-9). The Spirit also ensures that evil actions reap painful consequences. Even those who reject God cannot do

> *Every good gift and every perfect gift is from above, coming down from the Father of lights, with whom there is no variation or shadow due to change.*
>
> JAMES 1:17

anything they please; they can only do what God through the Spirit permits (Jer. 10:23).

The purpose or goal of the Spirit is to bring glory to God. Even the works of the Spirit among unbelievers are targeted at this goal. So He does not set up world circumstances or reveal aspects of God's work arbitrarily – it is all working together to turn hearts toward God and bring glory to God. And that, really, is what we should be about as well. We should pray for the Spirit to spread God's glory among unbelievers. Even in this fallen world we should look for truth and beauty, and then find ways to make it known. As we do this, we can be grateful that God the Spirit is at work there too, and thank Him for the privilege of joining His work.

15

How does the Holy Spirit help in the preaching of God's Word?

Probably all of us have been in one of those church services that felt dead. Whether it was our own hardheartedness or the lack of Holy Spirit power, something just felt off. And we have all been in church services where the Holy Spirit blew through the congregation with great power, igniting hearts with repentance and love for God. Sometimes we are among those whose lives have been changed – we've been pricked to the heart and prompted to respond. Such occasions are special acts of the Holy Spirit to illuminate the preaching of God's Word.

Jesus' parable of the Sower illustrates the difference between effectual and ineffectual preaching (Mt. 13:1-23). The good soil – which was soft and ready to receive the Word and produce a crop – is an example of the Holy Spirit at work. He opens hearts and prepares us to receive the Word of God and bear fruit. He replaces hearts of stone with hearts of flesh. Like the other works of the Spirit, this is a mysterious work, something that we cannot control or manufacture or predict. The Spirit blows where He wills, just like the wind, and often we know it only after it has happened.

We can tell when the Spirit has aided in the preaching of the Word because fruit is produced. A preacher may be able to fill the pews and inspire an emotional response through entertainment or manipulation or great oratorical skill, but if the Spirit is not present, there will be no lasting fruit. The congregants will return to their old ways by Wednesday, for the Word will not have penetrated their hearts to produce lasting change. If, however, the Spirit has visited us, we will see true repentance, changed lives, and people responding to Jesus in faith.

Although the Spirit cannot be controlled, He can be invited to empower our church services and the preaching of God's Word. We do this by bathing our services and church work in prayer, asking the Spirit to enter in. We approach all things with humility, asking the Spirit to correct us where we are wrong and guide us into the will

> *And we impart this in words not taught by human wisdom but taught by the Spirit, interpreting spiritual truths to those who are spiritual*
>
> 1 CORINTHIANS 2:13

of God. As servant-leaders, we make sure that we are walking closely with the Spirit and continually being filled up with Him so that His love and power can flow out of us to others.

Perhaps most importantly, pastors and service planners should focus on the Word of God, for this is what the Spirit has promised to illuminate for us. It is through the careful preaching of God's Word that the Spirit chooses to act to bring people to Jesus (Rom. 10:14). If the Spirit's goal is to glorify Christ, and if His chosen means for accomplishing that goal is Holy Scripture, then that should be the focus of our teaching and preaching as well. The great London preacher Charles Spurgeon once said that the purpose of preaching is to "make men tremble, make them sad, bring them to Jesus, and cause them to rejoice." When our preaching is Spirit-filled it will achieve all of these purposes, producing reverence, repentance, faith, and joy.

16

What is the unity of the Spirit? How can we have it?

As Jesus left the earth, His main concern was that the body of believers would be unified, one in purpose and mind. This is what He prayed for the night before He was crucified (Jn. 17). Today the total unity of the church seems like an impossible dream, but if Jesus Himself asked the Father for it, and then left the Holy Spirit to help us in this task, then surely it is not beyond our grasp.

In one sense, the unity of believers is a fact. Whether we feel like it or not, we are one in Christ, unified by a common faith into one baptism under one Father. Paul wrote, "For in one Spirit we were all baptized into one body – Jews or Greeks, slaves or free – and all were made to drink of one Spirit" (1 Cor. 12:13). God has made us members of one another, a body that supports one another and works together toward a common goal (Eph. 4:16). Realizing that unity is a work of God, not our own doing, can help us make Christian unity more of a living reality in our local body of believers.

Jesus wants the church to be unified for a purpose, and it isn't so that we can belong to a nice club of people who are like us and make us feel comfortable. The purpose of unity in the church is to proclaim the gospel. Jesus prayed, "That they may become perfectly one, so that the world may know that you sent me and loved them even as you loved me" (Jn. 17:23). Our like-mindedness stems from the fact that we stake our lives on the same tenets of our faith: we are sinners, Jesus made a way for us to be saved, and now it is our task to tell others this good news. When we are united around the truth of who God is, our love for Him, and our desire to serve Him, we will find it easier to work together to accomplish our huge task of making God known in the world.

> *Complete my joy by being of the same mind, having the same love, being in full accord and of one mind.*
>
> PHILIPPIANS 2:2

Of course, our experience in the church often is not one of unity but of disunity. We can find a seemingly infinite number of things to argue about, from the way the church building is decorated to the way we worship to the way we vote in an election. But unity is worth the effort. In fact, Paul tells us to make every effort to maintain our unity (Eph. 4:3) and also tells us the key to achieving it in the church: humility, after the example of Christ Himself (Phil. 2:1-11). Jesus took the humble position of a slave, and we should do no less.

Be willing to serve in lowly positions. Be humble with your opinions, realizing that you are not always right and that God has given His gifts and wisdom to the entire body, not you alone. Look to serve the interests of others. And be content with your status, having more concern for God's name and glory than your own. This is the way of Christ – the way that leads to the unity He prayed for us to experience and died for us to own.

17

What is spiritual warfare?

An old hymn says "Onward, Christian soldiers, marching as to war!" The hymn writer drew from the apostle Paul, who wrote "For we do not wrestle against flesh and blood, but against the rulers, against the authorities, against the cosmic powers over this present darkness, against the spiritual forces of evil in the heavenly places" (Eph. 6:12). We are in a spiritual battle, with forces of evil fighting against God to try to regain control over what He has already conquered.

The outcome of this cosmic war between good and evil has already been decided. Jesus defeated sin and death once and for all at the cross, so Satan is utterly defeated (1 Cor. 15:57; Col. 2:15). God wins! But Jesus hasn't yet returned to rule over His Kingdom in the new heaven and the new earth. Thus we live in an in-between time when Jesus has not yet fully displayed the victory that is His. Paul called this time an evil age (Gal. 1:4), and it's an era when there is a spiritual battle for souls. Satan uses every resource at his disposal to hang on to those who are his, while the victorious Christ conquers the hearts of those who belong to Him. This battle for the control of souls is what we call "spiritual warfare." It is fought not with physical weapons, but with spiritual weapons in the spiritual realm.

God Himself has equipped us for this battle. Paul describes the spiritual weapons at our disposal to fight this spiritual battle in Ephesians 6. We have the belt of truth, the breastplate of righteousness, shoes ready to share the gospel of peace, the shield of faith, the helmet of salvation, and the sword of the Spirit, which is the Word of God (vv. 14-17). Every day we are supposed to arm ourselves with these spiritual resources so we can fight off the temptations we face and help others find new life in Christ.

The weapon which undergirds all of these other spiritual resources is prayer in the Spirit. It is only through His power that we are able to proclaim the gospel and dispel darkness. Spiritual battles must be fought with spiritual resources, and the greatest spiritual resource of all is the Holy Spirit. What a comfort it is that our battle is the Lord's, and He will fight it for us with the power of the Spirit who lives in us. We are not alone to fight the darkness in our hearts or the darkness around us in the world. Through prayer we can wield our other weapons with confidence, knowing that the battle is already won and we are on the winning side.

Finally, be strong in the Lord and in the strength of his might. Put on the whole armor of God, that you may be able to stand against the schemes of the devil. For we do not wrestle against flesh and blood, but against the rulers, against the authorities, against the cosmic powers over this present darkness, against the spiritual forces of evil in the heavenly places.

Ephesians 6:10-12

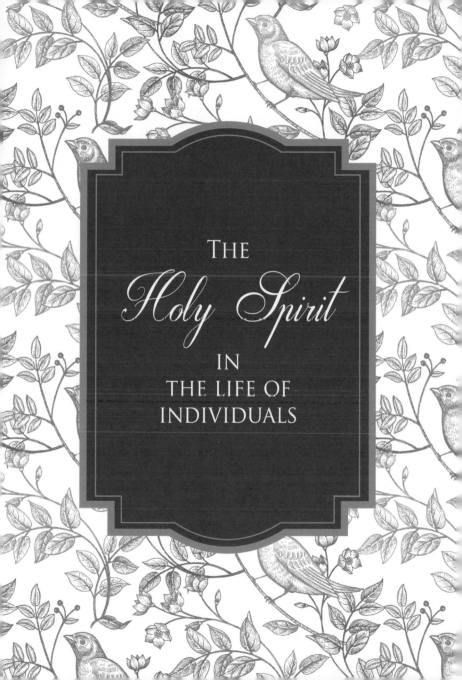

THE

Holy Spirit

IN
THE LIFE OF
INDIVIDUALS

18

What is the Holy Spirit's role in conversion?

Just as with the other works of God we've looked at so far, all three members of the Trinity are essential to conversion (the moment when we receive by faith the salvation Jesus earned for us at the cross and are regenerated, or "born again"). The apostle Paul described the different role each Person of the Godhead plays in conversion in Titus 3:4-7.

The Father created the loving plan to save us. Jesus cleansed us and justified us, making possible the pouring out of the Spirit. The Holy Spirit applies this salvation to us, executing God's plan by mediating to us and reproducing in us the fullness of redemption. He is the one who supernaturally regenerates and renews us so that we have spiritual life welling up inside us.

Let's start at the beginning, before we are saved by God's grace and awakened to new spiritual life. We start out as God's enemies. Apart from the Holy Spirit working in our minds and hearts we are opposed to God and totally unable to please Him (Heb. 11:6; Rom. 8:8).

Therefore, any spark of interest in the things of God, any insight into spiritual truth, any tiny bit of faith are workings of God's Spirit. He works from within to create in us the capacity for spiritual action. He opens our heart to spiritual things and then reveals them to us until we come to a clear enough understanding of what Christ has done for us that we can receive Him by faith. The Holy Spirit initiates and then we are able to respond with our acts of repentance and faith – acts the Bible describes as gifts of God (2 Tim. 2:25; Eph. 2:8).

Various theological systems approach this work of the Holy Spirit in conversion differently, but faithful theologians agree that there is some spiritual activity that precedes salvation. It is by God's grace that we are able to trust in Him, and the Holy Spirit is the One who works this grace into our hearts. The Spirit does a work in people's hearts before they are saved to bring about their salvation. God's call and our response are works of the Spirit.

The work of the Holy Spirit in conversion is yet another example of God's lavish grace. Even before we turned to Him, God was working in us. Our faith does not depend on us, who are so weak and fickle, but on God Almighty. And that also goes for our friends and family members who don't know Him. We may not see it yet, but the Spirit may already be working to soften their hearts toward the things of God, and at the right moment He will fan the spark of faith into a blazing fire. We can pray and witness with courage because conversion is the Spirit's work, not ours.

---

*God's love has been poured into our hearts through
the Holy Spirit who has been given to us.*

Romans 5:5

19

What does it mean to receive the Holy Spirit?

Though we might wish it, none of us had the power to choose where, when, or to whom we were born. We were utterly powerless in the matter. Our parentage is a mysterious gift from God. Jesus tells us that it's the same way with receiving new life in the Holy Spirit.

He told Nicodemus, "Unless one is born again he cannot see the kingdom of God" (Jn. 3:3). Then he specified that this is a birth of the Spirit: "Unless one is born of water and the Spirit, he cannot enter the kingdom of God" (v. 5). Finally, Jesus specified how this would take place: "The wind blows where it wishes, and you hear its sound, but you do not know where it comes from or where it goes. So it is with everyone who is born of the Spirit" (v. 8). In the same way that a baby does not chose the circumstances of his or her life, so also we are not able to control or predict the mysterious working of the Holy Spirit by which we receive eternal life in Christ.

The metaphor of new birth illustrates how life in Christ works. Just as a birth initiates new life, so also birth in the Spirit is the creation of new life. We become a new person with new desires and attitudes and ethics. Paul wrote, "If anyone is in Christ, he is a new creation. The old has passed away; behold, the new has come" (2 Cor. 5:17).

Furthermore, just as a baby has to grow and develop to become a mature adult, so also spiritual life involves growth. We start out as spiritual babies, with limited understanding of the things of God. At first we take in milk, relying on others to explain spiritual truths to us. Then we grow up to take solid food as we study the Bible for ourselves. The book of Hebrews explains this process: "Solid food is for the mature, for those who have their powers of discernment trained by constant practice to distinguish good from evil" (Heb. 5:14).

This growth from a spiritual baby to a mature adult is a supernatural process, initiated and sustained by the Holy Spirit. Just as a human baby looks like his or her biological parents, so also spiritual babies grow up to look more and more like their Father in heaven. There is a family likeness among the people of God. Those who are born of the Spirit begin to take on their Father's priorities and exhibit His characteristics. We also begin to look more and more like Jesus, our elder brother in the family of God (Heb. 2:11-12). We begin to love like He does, to serve like He does, and to trust our Father like He does. The best part is, because this is a work of the Holy Spirit, the results depend on Him and not on us. We work with the Spirit in the task, of course, but God has promised that He who began this good work in us will bring it to completion (Phil. 1:6).

*That which is born
of the flesh is flesh,
and that which is born
of the Spirit is spirit.*
JOHN 3:6

20

What does it mean to be born of the Holy Spirit?

In Acts 8 we read that the apostles were sent to Samaria to pray for the new believers there so that they would receive the Holy Spirit (Acts 8:14-17). These Samaritans were already believers. They "paid attention" (v. 6) and had "much joy" (v. 8) – both of which were elsewhere given as evidence of saving faith (Acts 16:14; 8:39). They believed (v. 12) and were baptized (v. 16). So at least in this case, the receiving of the Spirit was an event separate from conversion. Is this true today? Is there a second Spirit-directed experience after conversion and the indwelling of the Spirit? And is this accompanied by an outward sign such as speaking in tongues? There are widely divergent answers to these questions among various church denominations, and sometimes even in the same church.

Assuming that the Samaritans were believers prior to this experience of the Spirit "falling on" them does not mean that we should expect or require these to be separate events in the life of a believer today. At that time the Christian faith was new. Some Jewish believers were skeptical that non-Jews could become members of the household of faith. And so the Spirit was given at the laying on of the apostle's hands to convince Jews and non-Jews alike that anyone who believed in Jesus was now a full member of God's family (Acts 10:44-46; Eph. 2:11-22). The separation of personal conversion and the public receiving of the Spirit was a sign given in a special situation for a particular era as evidence of God's worldwide plan of salvation.

Repent and be baptized every one of you in the name of Jesus Christ for the forgiveness of your sins, and you will receive the gift of the Holy Spirit.

ACTS 2:38

In the book of Acts, every person who comes to faith is described as having a visible experience of the Holy Spirit. People knew a person had come to faith if he or she had experienced the Holy Spirit. That is why Paul asked the Ephesians, "Did you receive the Holy Spirit when you believed?" (Acts 19:2). He expected a person who had received the Holy Spirit to know it. In Paul's experience, after new converts received the Holy Spirit they did something that demonstrated the Spirit's presence – they spoke in tongues or prophesied or freely praised God or obeyed Him or boldly and powerfully witnessed to the death and resurrection of Jesus.

And so it is with us. Every one of us is promised that the Spirit will come upon us in power (Acts 1:8). We may not receive the particular gift of speaking in tongues or prophesying, but we will have a powerful experience of divine reality. The question, "did you receive the Spirit?" could just as well be worded "are you sorry for your sin?" or "do you have a desire to obey God?" or "are you filled with praise to God for who He is and what He has done?" or "do you have fresh hope and courage even in the face of great difficulty?" If the answer to any of these questions is yes, then you have indeed received the Holy Spirit.

21

What is the Holy Spirit's role in the gift of faith?

George Müller educated and provided for 10,024 orphans during his life, in addition to maintaining a busy preaching ministry and distributing 1.5 million New Testaments and over 285,000 Bibles. Müller had an astonishing outreach, but perhaps the most notable thing about his life is that he did all of this ministry through faith and prayer, with no regular salary or personal wealth to carry him along. When he had a need, he prayed, and God provided exactly what he needed exactly when he needed it.

A person like George Müller shows us what the gift of faith looks like. This is not saving faith – the trust that every believer places in Jesus for salvation, which is also a gift – but rather the special ability God gives through the Holy Spirit whereby certain people at certain times are empowered to live with unusual total dependence upon Him. Abraham displayed this gift when, although he had no earthly reason to hope that God would keep His promise to give him an heir, he nevertheless continued to hope (Rom. 4:18). We also see this gift at work in Mary's simple, childlike trust that God would do the impossible and conceive a child in her virgin womb (Lk. 1:38). Such faith goes beyond intellectual assent or human reason and simply believes enough to confidently trust in God even in seemingly impossible circumstances.

This gift of above-and-beyond faith comes from the Holy Spirit. It is not something we choose or conjure up in our own power. But even if we are not specially gifted with faith by the Spirit, each of us can and should grow in our faith. We can do this by looking for evidence of God's love. The more we study God's Word and witness the faithfulness of God in our lives and the lives of others, the more persuaded we will be that God is all-powerful and is working all things according to His perfect plan. Our vision of God will grow bigger, and we will know in our hearts as well as in our heads that He can do the impossible. We will have a firm conviction that God will do what He has promised, no matter how improbable or supernatural. And then we will act in accordance with our faith, taking bold risks for the Kingdom of God.

> *To each is given the manifestation of the Spirit for the common good. For to one is given through the Spirit ... faith.*
> 1 CORINTHIANS 12:7-9

The gift of faith is given to particular Christians for building up the body of Christ (1 Cor. 12:7-9). In other words, like all of God's gifts it is to be shared with others and used for the common good. Do you have a humble confidence that God can do anything and everything? Do you believe He will act when others only see the obstacles? If so, then fan the gift of faith by reading God's Word and listening to the faith stories of others, and then speak up with trust and courage when you sense God calling your family or church to do something almost impossible for the glory of Jesus Christ.

22

What is the Holy Spirit's role in repentance?

The Greek word for repentance, *metanoia*, refers to regretting a wrong view and changing to a right view. It literally means "to think again." This kind of "second thought" that the Bible has in mind is a change of heart that leads to a change of conduct. In this sense it is not primarily the onetime repentance that leads to salvation, but rather the ongoing practice of aligning our view with God's view and allowing that view to change our behavior. Repentance is a day-by-day, moment-by-moment turning away from sin and self toward God.

It is the presence of the Holy Spirit that brings about such repentance. The book of Acts describes it as being "cut to the heart" (Acts 2:37). Preachers often speak of the Holy Spirit's role in repentance as one of *conviction* – the inner voice of conscience that points out where we are straying from the path of righteousness. The Holy Spirit shines His holy light in our hearts so we can see our sin and are moved to do something about it.

Jesus described the Holy Spirit's role in repentance by saying, "And when he comes, he will convict the world concerning sin and righteousness and judgment" (Jn. 16:8). Jesus then went on to describe what this means. First, the Holy Spirit convicts us of the sin of unbelief. This is in keeping with His primary aim of glorifying Jesus. When we fail to see Jesus as He is and glorify Him as we ought, the Holy Spirit steps in to remind us of His greatness. Next the Spirit convicts us of righteousness by shining the brilliant light of God's perfection. When we see His purity, we become sorry for our sins and are moved to ask Him to clear away the darkness in our lives. Finally, the Spirit convicts us of judgment as a reminder that God is the victorious judge, and therefore we should take refuge in Him. When we come to Him for salvation and confess our sins, we are saved from His wrath and saved to life and goodness.

> *Repent therefore, and turn back, that your sins may be blotted out, that times of refreshing may come from the presence of the Lord.*
>
> ACTS 3:19-20

The conviction of the Spirit is God's kindness, for it leads us to repentance and true life in Christ.

The primary way the Spirit works to convict us and bring us to repentance is through the Word of God. The book of Hebrews compares the Bible to a double-edged sword for its ability to separate the thoughts and motives of the heart (Heb. 4:12). Scripture has the power to lay bare our hearts and cut away our sin because it is the sword of the Spirit (Eph. 6:17). These are not the words of mere men, but the words of God that are supernaturally illuminated by the Spirit of truth. Therefore it should not surprise us when we are moved to tears by our sinfulness and God's love as we read the pages of Scripture. In fact, if we are not moved then we are probably not reading it right!

23

What is the Holy Spirit's role in sanctification?

Every good gardener knows that in order to bring forth the best fruit, a tree needs to be pruned. The cutting away of diseased or unfruitful branches enables the healthy ones to use all of the plant's resources to produce juicy, beautiful fruit.

Season by season, year by year, the best branches are left and the plant grows stronger. In addition, the gardener might graft in new branches, adding new life to the original plant. The wild branches that don't belong are cut off, while the cultivated branches become stronger and bear fruit. But this process of creating the best possible tree only happens through wounding it. It is through violent cutting away that the tree grows strong.

Jesus used the metaphor of a gardener and a vine to illustrate how God works to sanctify us or make us more holy (Jn. 15). This is a work of all three members of the Trinity – God the Father, God the Son, and God the Holy Spirit are all described in Scripture as sanctifying agents in the life of a believer. But sanctification is the special province of the Spirit. He is the one who forms Christ in us and joins us to Christ (1 Pet. 1:2).

Just as the plant grows wild branches and the gardener grafts in cultivated ones, so it is with us. We have two natures warring within us. God made us a new creature at the moment of regeneration, but there is an ongoing process by which our spiritual life grows to replace our sin nature. Our disposition does not change overnight, but little by little we see the spiritual transformation.

We learn to be at peace where we used to be anxious. We learn to love where we used to hate. We learn to desire holiness where we used to love sin. This change of heart is the Spirit cutting away what is left of the old nature and grafting in new qualities – things like love and joy and peace and faith. But we should not expect that this process will be painless. We may be wounded, just as a tree is wounded by pruning and grafting, but it is for our good, so that we may bear fruit.

> "I am the vine; you are the branches. Whoever abides in me and I in him, he it is that bears much fruit, for apart from me you can do nothing."
>
> JOHN 15:5

This process of sanctification is Spirit-initiated and Spirit-directed, but we participate in it as well. When Jesus used this metaphor He urged His followers to "remain" or "abide" in Him (Jn. 15:4). What does this mean? It means that we draw our life from His life. We stay close to Him through prayer, through studying the Bible, and through receiving the sacrament of communion. We learn from Him and imitate Him. We cut away the sinful deeds of the flesh so that the life of the spirit can flourish in us. These are the ways that we work out our salvation, even as God works His salvation into us (Phil. 2:12-13).

24

What is the Holy Spirit's role in the life of a nonbeliever?

Most of us have loved ones who don't seem to have any interest in the things of God. They shut down every conversation we try to start about spiritual things, and their lifestyle seems totally godless, at least as far as we are able to see. We wonder if the Holy Spirit has anything to do with them. We've already talked about how the Spirit works in the world and in the process of someone coming to faith in Jesus. But what about in the life of a nonbeliever who does not seem to be seeking God at the moment? Does the Spirit have any role in their lives?

This is a hard question to answer. The Holy Spirit certainly has the power to restrain evil in the world, which includes keeping individuals from actions that would bring greater harm. Many mothers tell stories about how the Spirit kept a wayward child from harm even during years when he or she was running away from God. On the other hand, the Bible tells us that at some point God gives people over to their sin. The Spirit removes His protective hand from people when they continually rebel against God. Usually when the Bible talks about God "giving people over" to their sin it is a final and irrevocable turning away from God, and they never return to Him

(Ps. 81:12; Rom. 1:24). Of course, we can never tell whether God is letting people hit rock bottom so they will turn to Him, or whether He is giving them over to their desires once and for all. Our job is simply to keep telling them about the love of Jesus and praying for them.

For this reason I bow my knees before the Father … that according to the riches of his glory he may grant you to be strengthened with power through his Spirit in your inner being, so that Christ may dwell in your hearts through faith.

EPHESIANS 3:14, 16-17

Maybe the most helpful verse about what the Spirit does in the life of a nonbeliever is one we've already looked at. John 16:8 reads, "[the Spirit] will convict the world concerning sin and righteousness and judgment." The word for *convicts* is a judicial term that describes how the Holy Spirit convinces people – everyone in the whole world – of the existence of right and wrong and ultimately of the existence of God. In other words, the Spirit works in the minds and heart of nonbelievers to reveal to them the holy love and righteous justice of God.

There are two applications here for our lives. First, it is both humbling and challenging to note that the Spirit's presence – including His presence in *our* lives – should affect those around us. The holiness, goodness, and love the Spirit produces in us should convict the world concerning sin and righteousness and judgment. Furthermore, we should be active witnesses to God's love. Even when we are shut down time after time, even when our words seem to have little or no effect, even when we have given up hope that our loved ones will ever turn to Jesus in faith – even then we should reach out to them and share how God has helped us. No one can say when and where the Spirit will move; maybe today is the day.

25

What is the Holy Spirit's role in evangelism?

You've finally gotten up the nerve to share the love of Jesus with a neighbor. Your palms are sweaty, your heart is racing, you open your mouth … and nothing goes quite as planned. You bumble along in embarrassment and walk away wondering if you just totally blew it.

Did you read the signals wrong? Was this the wrong time to share? Did you just turn them off to spiritual things? Will the mistakes you made end up making it harder for your neighbor to come to Christ? In those moments, we sometimes wonder where the Holy Spirit is. We know He's at work in the heart of someone who comes to Him in faith, but what about those times when we witness and nothing seems to be happening?

The first thing to note is that you were not alone during that difficult conversation. We have the promise straight from the lips of Jesus that the Holy Spirit is powerfully working through believers to witness about Him. Jesus said, "Do not be anxious how you are to speak or what you are to say, for what you are to say will be given to you in that hour. For it is not you who speak, but the Spirit of your

Father speaking through you" (Mt. 10:19-20). Even if we do not have the success we wish and pray for, or we stumble over our words and don't quite get it right, the Spirit is at work in our witnessing.

Even more importantly, the results are not up to us. There is a clear-cut division of labor in the process of evangelism. We are commanded to bear witness, telling others about what God has done in Christ Jesus. This involves praying for boldness, speaking out with courage, and trusting in God. God uses what we do and makes it effective. All the growth, all the conversion, all the power are on God's side of the equation. The Holy Spirit is the One who convicts and brings to repentance. We can't control it, we can't manipulate it, we can't wish it into being: spiritual life only comes through the power of the Spirit. Even if we have success in evangelism and lead many people to the Lord, this is not our doing, it is a gift from God.

This gives us the freedom to be bold in our evangelism. We can go ahead and have that conversation with our neighbor. We don't need to be nervous about it because we know that God is with us. We should do our best to plan ahead so we can clearly present the gospel, and we should pray for the Spirit's help before and during our conversation. But any effort can be used by God, and He will bring forth new life in our neighbors at the appointed time. Our only job is to speak up about what God has done, and then watch to see what God will do. We do the presenting, but the Holy Spirit does the persuading.

"But you will receive power when the Holy Spirit has come upon you, and you will be my witnesses in Jerusalem and in all Judea and Samaria, and to the end of the earth."

Acts 1:8

26

How does the Holy Spirit comfort believers?

It's easy to envy the disciples for their proximity to Jesus. How amazing – if sometimes puzzling – it must have been to walk by the Savior's side for three years. But Jesus promised that He has left us with an even better gift, the Holy Spirit, who is to us all that Jesus was to the disciples, and more. Jesus said, "I will ask the Father, and he will give you another Helper, to be with you forever, even the Spirit of truth" (John 14:16-17). The Spirit is *another* comforter, of which Jesus was the first. The word Jesus used for comforter is *paraclete*, which literally means "called to" or "called beside." It connotes both comfort and legal advocacy. The Holy Spirit is our guide, counselor, and friend who walks beside us each moment of our lives, and that is indeed a great comfort.

The first way the Spirit comforts us is with His presence. When we are troubled or experiencing grief, what we most want is for someone to sit with us and hold our hand. This is the ministry of presence – simply being with someone in their grief, not trying to solve their problems or tell them how they should feel. The Holy Spirit lives inside each believer, so in all our trials and griefs God is there.

The Spirit also comforts us with teaching. Jesus said, "But the Helper, the Holy Spirit … will teach you all things and bring to your remembrance all that I have said to you" (Jn. 14:26). Later Jesus spoke of the Spirit guiding us into truth (Jn. 16:13). The Holy Spirit supernaturally leads us to understand the things of God – specifically, the truths He has revealed in the Scripture He inspired. He instills them into our inner being so that we know them deep in our hearts as well as intellectually with our minds. This is a very practical help to us as we try to choose right behavior and navigate decisions about which path to take.

The Spirit is also our advocate (1 Jn. 2:1; Rom. 8:27). He speaks for us, pleading our case before the Father. This is a comfort because it reassures us that our sins were already judged on the cross, and therefore we stand forgiven, declared righteous. Our position as God's child is secure; our future in heaven is guaranteed; and each time we pray the Spirit Himself is helping us to pray in God's will so that our prayers will be answered.

These comforting ministries of the Holy Spirit are wonderful gifts, but perhaps best of all is the peace He gives us. There is an unexplainable peace that exudes from a believer even in the face of deep suffering. It is more than just the confidence we have that God loves us and will do good for us – it is a deep calm that is unruffled by any circumstance. And this peace is ours thanks to the Holy Spirit's presence in our hearts.

"I will ask the Father, and he will give you another Helper, to be with you forever, even the Spirit of truth, whom the world cannot receive, because it neither sees him nor knows him. You know him, for he dwells with you and will be in you."

JOHN 14:16-17

27

What does it mean that I am a temple of the Holy Spirit?

The Israelites had been delivered from slavery in Egypt one year before, but now understandably the people were feeling a little insecure. What would happen to them next? Would God still be with them? At this crucial juncture in their history, God in His mercy set up a visible reminder of His presence and protection. The Tabernacle was a tent that would be moved with the people every time God led them to a new place. The people could come to worship God in this place, and He would meet with the spiritual leaders there. Best of all, God's glorious presence was in the Tabernacle, right among His people (Ex. 29:45-46).

After the time of David, when the nation of Israel was more permanently settled in Jerusalem, God instructed them to build the Temple. This beautiful building would be the long-term residence of God among His people, a place where they could come to meet with the holy Redeemer. Like the Tabernacle, the Temple had a special place, called the holy of holies, where God's presence dwelt. It was separated from the rest of the Temple by a thick curtain, and only the high priest could enter there, and only once a year. The holy God was separated from the sinfulness of humanity.

When Jesus died, a new era began. At the moment of Jesus' death, the curtain separating the holy of holies was miraculously torn from top to bottom (Mt. 27:50-51). This was the sign that we are no longer separated from God's holiness by our sin. Jesus had made a way for His people to be forgiven and to speak with God face-to-face.

When Jesus returned to heaven, He left the Holy Spirit to dwell in our hearts. In effect, we have become God's holy place. As the apostle Paul wrote, "Your body is a temple of the Holy Spirit within you, whom you have from God ... So glorify God in your body" (1 Cor. 6:19-20). In these short verses we see an important truth. Each Christian is a home for God's glory here on earth. What the Tabernacle and the Temple were to God's people in the Old Testament, our bodies have become. God's presence is in us. We can experience communion with Him every moment of our lives. And we are conduits of His glory to the world, the means by which He lives with and loves His people.

Or do you not know that your body is a temple of the Holy Spirit within you, whom you have from God? You are not your own, for you were bought with a price. So glorify God in your body.

1 CORINTHIANS 6:19-20

What does this mean for us? First of all, it is a responsibility. We should seek to live pure and holy lives, for we dare not defile the house of God with petty sins or unholy passions. If you would not do or say something in church, you should not do it at all, for you *are* the church – the holy place where God is. Secondly, it is an enormous privilege.

God indwells us through the Spirit so that we can serve others. We should be so filled with the Spirit that our presence brings peace and love to everyone we meet. It is our privilege to let God's glory freely flow out of us, like light streaming through the stained-glass windows of a beautiful sanctuary.

28

What is the Spirit's role in worship?

Churches often advertise their worship services based on style or entertainment value. They use words like "dynamic," "enthusiastic," and "fresh." They may even use the word "Spirit-filled." In all of this branding, sometimes we are so busy concentrating on our experience of worship or the attractiveness of our church's worship service that we miss the objective truth about the Holy Spirit's role in our worship.

The truth is, the Spirit is intimately involved in all true worship. The Bible consistently defines worship as an act of devotion performed by those who are part of God's covenant family through faith. Apart from the regenerating work of the Holy Spirit that seals us as part of God's family, we cannot truly worship God. We may sing the songs, we may listen to the sermon, we may even pray, but if we have not received salvation through Christ's work on the cross, we are not worshiping in spirit or truth (Jn. 4:24). Only those who have a relationship with God through Jesus can rightly worship Him.

The Spirit is also involved in worship by drawing believers together in a community. Though we are individually temples of the Holy Spirit, we are being built together into a larger temple. Peter wrote, "You yourselves like living stones are being built up as a spiritual house, to be a holy priesthood, to offer spiritual sacrifices acceptable to God through Jesus Christ" (1 Pet. 2:5). Practically speaking, this means that the primary context for worship is with other believers.

Be filled with the Spirit, addressing one another in psalms and hymns and spiritual songs, singing and making melody to the Lord with your heart, giving thanks always and for everything to God the Father in the name of our Lord Jesus Christ.

EPHESIANS 5:18-20

The Spirit's gifts are given to the body as a whole, so we are best able to worship God together, where we can benefit from each other's gifts. Biblically speaking, personal worship honors God, but corporate worship is even better because it is a more complete expression of God's glory.

Back to that open-ended term "Spirit-filled worship". Often people use this term to mean worship that is particularly emotional, perhaps a bit informal, and often utilizing the gift of tongues. But the Bible does not limit the Holy Spirit to a certain style of worship service. Every time Christians gather together to rehearse salvation history in Scripture and song and to praise God's glorious name, that is worship. It may or may not include music. It may or may not move us emotionally.

True worship that pleases God is mindful, heart-filled praise to the Savior that leads to a life of obedience and love to Him. And Spirit-filled worship is any act of praise and devotion that is motivated by the presence and power of the Holy Spirit that God has promised to His people.

73

29

What is the baptism of the Spirit?

One of the two sacraments of the Christian church is baptism (communion, also called the Lord's Supper, is the other). Baptism is the sprinkling of or immersion into water as a symbolic representation of being united with Christ in His death and resurrection. But when we're talking about the Holy Spirit, there is another kind of baptism – baptism *of* (or *with* or *into*) the Spirit. What is this baptism, and what difference does it make in the daily life of a Christian?

Being baptized with the Holy Spirit is a divine act whereby Christians are initiated into union with Christ. It is the inner spiritual reality that we portray sacramentally when we baptize believers with water. John the Baptist first foretold the baptism of the Spirit when he said, "He who is mightier than I is coming. ... He will baptize you with the Holy Spirit and fire" (Lk. 3:16). Jesus also predicted this spiritual baptism in Acts 1:5, and then we read about the first time it occurred, at Pentecost, in Acts 2. The dramatic experience of the first Christians is evidence that baptism with the Spirit is a powerful event in the life of a believer, with visible results as believers grow in their faith and begin to serve others in the pattern of Christ.

For believers today, baptism with the Holy Spirit typically occurs simultaneously with regeneration. Paul makes it clear that this is an event that takes place at salvation in his letter to the Corinthians: "In one Spirit we were all baptized into one body – Jews or Greeks, slaves or free – and all were made to drink of one Spirit" (1 Cor. 12:13). Baptism with the Spirit is the normative experience of every believer, not just of a few super-Christians. Because baptism with the Spirit is the experience of every believer, it is not synonymous with the gift of speaking in tongues, which is only given to some Christians (1 Cor. 12:30).

"I have baptized you with water, but he will baptize you with the Holy Spirit."

MARK 1:8

The baptism of the Holy Spirit has ongoing implications in our daily life. On an individual level, it is the basis for our union with Christ. Through the Spirit's baptism, Jesus becomes real to us and we sense His glory and love. We are able not only to believe the gospel in our heads, but also to act on our faith with our hearts and hands. On a corporate level, baptism in the Spirit enables us to be united as the worldwide church. We have a supernatural union around the truth of the gospel through the work of the Spirit, and this allows us to work together as an expression of the Kingdom of God.

We have a bond with other believers, even those with whom we seem to have nothing else in common – a bond that is both objectively real and subjectively felt. The baptism of the Spirit makes us one family.

30

What does it mean to be sealed with the Holy Spirit?

When you make a big purchase, such as a house or car, you are often required to pay a deposit or "earnest money." This sum is a small portion of the total cost, but it shows the seller that you are serious about making the purchase.

Making the down payment guarantees not only that you will pay the rest of the total, but also that the seller will not sell it to someone else in the meantime. It is a legally binding agreement that protects both parties.

The Bible says that the Holy Spirit is the "guarantee" or "down payment" on our eternal inheritance in Christ (2 Cor. 1:22; 5:5; Eph. 1:13-14; 4:30). The Greek word is *arrhabon*, which means "pledge." This pledge is a legally binding promise that guarantees the rest of the promises. In spiritual terms, God placed the Spirit in our hearts at the moment we received salvation as a seal that assures us that the rest of His promises are coming to us. We have a down payment on the eternal salvation that is ours in Christ.

The seal of the Holy Spirit marks us as belonging to God in an everlasting covenant relationship, so we can know with certainty that we will be with Him forever. Once the down payment of the Spirit has been made, nothing can separate us from God's love, not even Satan and the powers of hell or our own sinfulness (Rom. 8:38-39). God has promised that no one can snatch us out of His hand (Jn. 10:28-30).

We have been adopted into God's family, and that is an irrevocable change of relationship (Rom. 8:15; Gal. 4:6). In the meantime, the seal of the Holy Spirit guarantees that God will continue to sanctify us and grow our faith. Once that process is set in motion, God the Spirit will continue it until the day of eternity.

How can we know that we have indeed been sealed with the Holy Spirit? This is an objective fact that may or may not be accompanied by feelings of assurance. But even if you sometimes doubt God's love or

In him you also, when you heard the word of truth, the gospel of your salvation, and believed in him, were sealed with the promised Holy Spirit, who is the guarantee of our inheritance until we acquire possession of it, to the praise of his glory.

Ephesians 1:13-14

even His existence, if you have turned to Him in repentance and faith, the Holy Spirit is living inside you. Over time, you will exhibit more and more of the fruit of the Spirit (Gal. 5:22-23). You will discover that the Spirit has given you gifts for building up the body of Christ. You will have an increasing desire to know God. You will come to hate sin and long for holiness, and as a result you will feel sorrow over your sin and repent of it. You will love God's people and look forward to worshiping with them. You will have a growing sense that you are God's child and He is your loving Father. This is all part of the sealing work of the Holy Spirit.

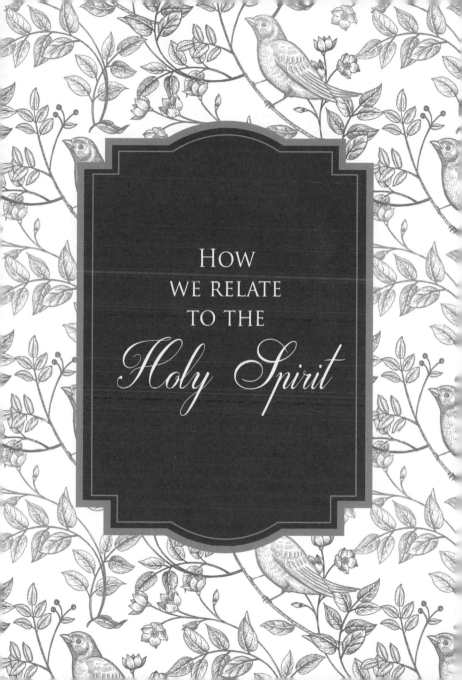

HOW
WE RELATE
TO THE
Holy Spirit

31

What is the Holy Spirit's role in prayer?

Christians don't always know how to take advantage of the privilege of prayer. We know we should pray more often, but we aren't sure how. When asked, we can't always come up with an intelligent answer for why we should pray. Perhaps this is the reason most Christians struggle to keep a consistent prayer life. The good news is that we are not alone in this endeavor, because the Holy Spirit is our helper in prayer, as He is in so many other aspects of the Christian life.

It's no exaggeration to say that all true prayer is wrought in the soul by the Holy Spirit. The Spirit makes prayer possible in the first place, for He is the one who applies salvation to our hearts so that we have a right to pray boldly and confidently to God as our loving Father (Rom. 8:16). The faith that moves us to pray is also a gift of the Spirit. We couldn't and wouldn't pray apart from the work of the Spirit in our lives. But the Spirit's help in prayer goes far beyond the mere ability to pray.

The Spirit gives us the words to pray. We've talked already about how the Spirit teaches us about Christ, and that same leading carries over into our prayer lives as well. If we don't know how to pray, we should ask the Spirit – He will be our teacher. He will place burdens on our hearts for intercession. He will wake us up at night with an overwhelming urge to pray for a loved one in need. He will reveal Scriptures to pray. And He will instill in us a deep current of close relationship with God that helps us understand the will of God so we can pray for the right things.

Sometimes our need is so great that we have no words, and the Spirit helps us then, too. Romans 8:26-27 tells us, "the Spirit helps us in our weakness. For we do not know what to pray for as we ought, but the Spirit himself intercedes for us with groanings too deep for words. And he who searches hearts knows what is the mind of the Spirit, because the Spirit intercedes for the saints according to the will of God."

This promise is a deep encouragement for those times when our problems are just too big for us to handle. We don't know how the problem can possibly be solved, or even what to pray for, but the Spirit who knows the will of God steps in and intercedes on our behalf with supernatural sighs that move the heart of God.

Likewise the Spirit helps us in our weakness. For we do not know what to pray for as we ought, but the Spirit himself intercedes for us with groanings too deep for words.

ROMANS 8:26

If prayer is hard for you, take heart. The Spirit will be your teacher and guide as you pray. All you have to do is start by asking for His help, and He will give you the words and the heart to pray.

32

Should we pray to the Holy Spirit?

The Holy Spirit's role is to glorify Jesus by leading us to an understanding of how His death and resurrection enable us to have a relationship with God the Father. For this reason, the usual pattern of prayer is for us to pray to the Father, in the name of the Son, through the power of the Holy Spirit.

In other words, we rely on the Holy Spirit's supernatural work to give us the inclination and the words to pray, and we rely on Jesus for the right to approach the throne of God with our praises and petitions, but most of our prayers are directed to God the Father. This fits with the Biblical model of how Jesus and Paul prayed, as well as the Lord's Prayer, which serves as the primary pattern for our prayers (Mt. 6:9). With only one notable exception (Mk. 15:34), Jesus always prayed to the Father when He prayed (e.g., Lk. 23:46).

But is it ever right to pray directly to the Holy Spirit, inviting Him to blow through a gathering of believers with power, or enable us to make right decisions, or to understand the Word of God? It is in keeping with the role of the Holy Spirit to occasionally pray to Him. He is, after all, God. We can invoke His presence and ask Him to enact the will of God with power. We can invite Him to do what He does and promises to do – powerfully bear witness to Jesus, illuminate Scripture, and create new life so that sinners are born into God's family. However, because it is the Spirit's desire to glorify the Son, most of our prayers should not be directed to the Holy Spirit.

Scripture teaches us to pray to the Father in the name of the Son, and the Spirit works in the background to give life to our prayers. The Spirit should not be the primary object of our prayers, nor does He want to be, for that is not His role.

> *But you, beloved, building yourselves up in your most holy faith and praying in the Holy Spirit, keep yourselves in the love of God.*
>
> JUDE 20-21

The Biblical model is to pray *in* or *with* the Spirit. We are urged to pray "at all times in the Spirit, with all prayer and supplication" (Eph. 6:18). The word *in* can be translated "by means of," "with the help of," or "in the sphere of." All of these things should be true about our prayers. Regardless of what we are praying about, we should be praying in concert with the Spirit, by means of His help, and according to His wisdom. In other words, the Spirit should be leading our prayers.

He is the one who teaches us how to pray and what to pray for. He motivates us to pray, lends supernatural groanings "too deep for words" (Rom. 8:26) to our prayers, and then leads us in praying for the Father's will. Which member of the Godhead we pray to does not matter as much as that we pray with the Spirit, in the name of Jesus, and for the will of God.

33

What is the role of the Holy Spirit in making life decisions?

Christians often agonize over the big decisions that we face in life. Sometimes we agonize over the little decisions, too. We want to do God's will, but we wonder if we are correctly discerning what His will is. Should I marry this person, or is my apprehension a sign from God that this isn't His plan?

Should I take that job or wait for something more ministry-oriented or better suited to my experience or desires? If I make the wrong choice, will that set off a whole series of events that will take my entire life off track? The good news is that the Holy Spirit's work in a believer ensures that if we are seeking God's will, we will find it. Our route to get there may appear circuitous, but anyone who is truly trying to obey God in life decisions will find the right path.

We have already talked about how the Spirit teaches us the truth, including the truth we find in God's Word (Jn. 14:26). He is the source of all wisdom for daily life. Even Job's sometimes misguided friends knew this, for they told him, "It is the spirit in man, the breath of the Almighty, that makes him understand. It is not the old who are wise, nor the aged who understand what is right" (Job 32:8-9). So if we want to be wise or to make a right decision, we should ask God and then trust that He will reveal His will to us through the Holy Spirit (James 1:5). That is the first step.

Discerning the will of God is not a passive process. We are not simply to sit in the presence of God and wait for the Holy Spirit to speak in an audible voice. Most likely that will never happen. God has given us minds, and He expects us to use them. So after we have prayed about a matter, we should engage our minds in the process of discerning the will of God. Study Scripture so that you are steeped in the truth, and then apply its overall wisdom to your life decisions. Consider as well how a particular decision fits with your life goal of loving and serving the Lord.

If any of you lacks wisdom, let him ask God, who gives generously to all without reproach, and it will be given him.

JAMES 1:5

Ask mature Christians – especially people who know you well – what they think about the decision before you.

These are all resources that the Holy Spirit may use to guide you. Yet you may try all of these tactics and still be unsure what to do. This is where faith comes in. As you walk forward in the presence of the Spirit, you can trust that God will guide you.

We all make mistakes, including bad choices, but God has the power to get us back on track. He will sovereignly direct circumstances so that you can fulfill His calling in your life. Your past does not limit His future for you. In the final analysis, if you're obeying God's commands and seeking to glorify God through your life, the particulars will sort themselves out.

34

What is blasphemy against the Holy Spirit?

When Jesus cast out a demon that was causing a man to be deaf and mute (Mt. 12:22-32; Mk. 3:22-29), the crowd began to wonder if He was the long-awaited Messiah. Their musing angered the Pharisees, and so the Pharisees took their opposition to Jesus to a new low and accused Him of driving out demons by the power of Beelzebul. Jesus first refuted their argument using the logic that a kingdom divided against itself cannot stand, and then He declared that the Pharisees had just committed an unpardonable sin. Jesus said, "Every sin and blasphemy will be forgiven people, but the blasphemy against the Spirit will not be forgiven" (Mt. 12:31).

What is this unforgivable sin, and how can we be sure that we have not committed it? Some people are tormented by the fear that they have done something unforgiveable, so it is important for us to know the answer to these questions.

In general terms, blasphemy is defiant irreverence or a particularly flagrant degradation of the things of

God. Attributing evil to God or profaning something that God has declared sacred are two forms of blasphemy.

The Pharisees' words against Jesus were particularly heinous because they had just witnessed the power of the Holy Spirit at work in the miracles of Jesus. They could see that this was the work of God, and yet they claimed that He was doing these things in the power of Satan. Thus they were publicly and permanently rejecting the Messiah to His face. In so doing, they were also rejecting the Spirit who anointed Jesus to be the Messiah. Mark is very clear that their words were blasphemy against the Holy Spirit because "they were saying, 'He has an unclean spirit'" (Mk. 3:30). Thus blasphemy against the Holy Spirit is a specific type of blasphemy that consists of an ongoing verbal accusation that the works of God are the works of Satan. The hallmark of the unpardonable sin of blasphemy against the Holy Spirit is a willful, ongoing rejection of the work of Jesus Christ by someone who ought to know better.

Once we understand the meaning of blasphemy against the Holy Spirit, we can see that it is not a sin believers are able to commit. The only "unpardonable sin" is willfully choosing to deny the saving work of Jesus. Of course, if we willfully resist the Spirit's conviction of sin, righteousness, and judgment and continue to be unrepentant even at the moment of death, we will not be pardoned. As Jesus said, "whoever believes in the Son has eternal life; whoever does not obey the Son shall not see life, but the wrath of God remains on him" (Jn. 3:36). As long as we have life and breath, we have the opportunity to repent of our sin. When we do so, we are responding to the Spirit (the opposite of blaspheming Him!) and will receive pardon for sin and the free gift of eternal life.

"All that the Father gives me will come to me, and whoever comes to me I will never cast out."

JOHN 6:37

35

What does it mean to keep in step with the Spirit?

When Paul wrote to the church in Galatia, he used strong words to call them back to the gospel of grace. They had begun to rely on adherence to the Law to save them, rather than the finished work of Christ on the cross. At the crux of Paul's admonition for grace-based Christianity is that Christians need to keep in step with the Spirit. He wrote, "If we live by the Spirit, let us also keep in step with the Spirit" (Gal. 5:25).

In other words, once we have received the Spirit and been born again, we must learn how to follow Him. The Greek word for "keep in step" is a military term that refers to following orders. When soldiers march or run in formation, they have to keep in step with their commanding officer. They may not know where they are going or how they are going to get there, but that isn't important because their only job at that moment is to keep in step. As long as they time their footsteps right, the *where* and the *how* will take care of themselves. Likewise, the Holy Spirit keeps us in line so we can keep in step with God's commands. As we follow the rise and fall of everything the Spirit teaches us, particularly through Scripture, we will get to where our Commanding Officer is leading us.

The implication in Paul's command to keep in step with the Spirit is that it is all too easy to fall out of step. We slow down a bit, resisting God's will because it's harder than we want it to be. Or we veer to the right or to the left, thinking in our pride that we know a better destination or a more interesting route. We get distracted and lose the rhythm of obedience. Or we try to run ahead of God's commands, adding to them our own works of righteousness. There are so many ways to get out of step with the Spirit.

If we live by the Spirit, let us also keep in step with the Spirit.

GALATIANS 5:25

How, then, can we keep in step with the Spirit? Certainly there is discipline involved. Soldiers have to train their bodies to march and their minds to follow orders. Likewise, we need the disciplines of Bible reading, prayer, church attendance, and the sacraments so that we can hear and heed the Spirit's commands. There is also a corporate aspect of keeping in step with the Spirit. Soldiers marching in formation need to pay attention to one another and help each other follow their leader, and we should do the same thing in our Christian walk. As we follow the Spirit's cadence, we can link arms with brothers and sisters in the faith who are fading and help them take the next step. If we grow weary, we can rely on those around us to bolster our faith. And for those who come after us, our footsteps of faith mark the path to show them where to go.

36

What does it mean to be filled with the Spirit?

The Holy Spirit is so crucial to our spiritual growth that it is natural for those who have been baptized with the Spirit to desire even more of Him – what the Bible calls being filled with the Spirit. The apostle Paul contrasted being filled with wine against being filled with the Spirit (Eph. 5:18).

If you consider some of the reasons people drink alcohol to excess, this analogy yields rich insight. People may drink to be exhilarated, to gain confidence, to alleviate pain, to enhance their mood, or for camaraderie. All these things the Holy Spirit does – only He does it in ways that are life-giving rather than destructive.

The filling of the Holy Spirit should not be confused with the indwelling of the Spirit. The Holy Spirit lives within all believers from the moment of regeneration, just as Jesus promised (Jn. 14:16). The Spirit is always present in our lives to convicts us, comfort us, and guarantee that we belong to God.

Being filled with the Spirit is a matter of giving the Spirit full sway over our whole being, allowing Him total access to our hearts and lives so He can do His work of convicting and training us in righteousness.

It is possible to be a true Christian but stifle the Spirit's work, whether through stubborn disobedience or lack of cooperation. But if we invite Him to fill us, we will be increasingly transformed into the image of Jesus Christ. We will have a growing desire to read Scripture and do what it says. We will have more intimate access to God through prayer. We will bear the fruit of the Spirit in our lives (Gal. 5:22-23). And we will be more effective in our work and witness for the gospel.

Paul explains that worship is both a pathway to and an outflow of being filled with the Spirit. He exhorts us to "be filled with the Spirit, addressing one another in psalms and hymns and spiritual songs, singing and making melody to the Lord with your heart, giving thanks always and for everything to God the Father in the name of our Lord Jesus Christ" (Eph. 5:18-20). As we worship God we will be filled with the Spirit in many different ways, and we will overflow with grateful praise for God's goodness.

How can we be filled with the Spirit? The first step is to ask for His overflowing presence. Pray to be filled with the Spirit for the glory of God. Then make room for Him through humble submission, obeying God and bowing before Him in wholehearted devotion. At the same time, refuse to put up any obstacles to the Spirit's work. When we ruthlessly uproot sin from our lives, discarding our idols and our misplaced passions, we make room for the Spirit to fill us up. He will fill us – to overflowing – with spiritual life that spills over into the lives those around us.

> *When they had prayed, the place in which they were gathered together was shaken, and they were all filled with the Holy Spirit and continued to speak the word of God with boldness.*
>
> ACTS 4:31

37

What does it mean to quench or grieve the Holy Spirit?

Before going to bed, experienced campers douse the campfire with water to quench the flame. They want to be sure that no spark can accidentally burst back to life while they sleep. Sometimes we do the same thing with the Holy Spirit's fire in our lives – we smother it. There are two commands against this in Paul's letters: "Do not grieve the Holy Spirit of God, by whom you were sealed for the day of redemption" (Eph. 4:30) and "Do not quench the Spirit" (1 Thess. 5:19). What does it mean for us to quench or grieve the Spirit, and how can we avoid doing so?

The first thing to note is that God is sovereign. We may quench, stifle, or grieve the Spirit, but ultimately we cannot act outside of His sovereign will. The Holy Spirit is able to override even our most self-destructive tendencies to bring us to repentance and restoration.

When Paul speaks of grieving the Holy Spirit, it is in the sense of a loving father who is moved by his child's sin. The parent sees the logical consequences of the path his child is on and is sorrowful over the pain his child will have to endure. Such grief is a tender and delicate emotion that is designed to arouse repentance – not something born of anger or judgment. When we sin, the Spirit is sorrowful for the harm our sin will bring to our souls.

God is jealous for our love, and therefore He is grieved when we give our devotion to something else. And He is grieved by our unbelief, for He knows we are only hurting ourselves by refusing to submit to His holy will.

Quenching the Spirit is stifling the flame He puts in our hearts. Our faith cannot be extinguished, but we can lessen the Spirit's influence over our lives through our own sinful choices. One way we do this is by despising His supernatural work (1 Thess. 5:19-20). When we disdain the Word of God or the works of God, we are quenching the Spirit. Another way we quench the Spirit is by failing to worship God, or to spend time with Him in prayer (Eph. 5:18-19). Our grateful praise and humble adoration of God makes room for the Spirit to fill us, and likewise our hardheartedness stifles His presence in us until we almost lose the ability to hear His voice. We can also quench the Spirit by resisting His work in our lives, either refusing to repent when we know we need to, resisting the fruit He bears in us, or neglecting to use the gifts He has given us.

Do not grieve the Holy Spirit of God, by whom you were sealed for the day of redemption.
Ephesians 4:30

The Holy Spirit longs to fill us and use us for the glory of God. We can either work with that process or hinder it through the choices we make about what we fill our minds and hearts with and how we act. Do your habits and attitudes help or hinder the Spirit's work in your life? Are you grieving the Spirit, or causing Him to rejoice?

38

What does it mean to be controlled by the Spirit?

Most of us recoil at the idea of being controlled by anyone or anything. We fancy ourselves autonomous beings, masters of our own fate, lords of our dominions. But the truth is that we are all controlled by something. We are born under the rule of sin, subject to its demands and enchained by our evil desires. Our only hope of liberation is Jesus, who died to save us from our slavery to sin and bring us into the domain of the Kingdom of God, where we are controlled not by our evil desires but by the Holy Spirit.

The contrast between the rule of Satan and the rule of God through the Holy Spirit is outlined in Romans 8. Not every translation uses the word "control," but the idea is still woven throughout. Those who are controlled or led by the sinful nature are focused on their own desires and passions. They are spiritually dead and hostile to God, and thus unable to please

Him. They have no hope and are destined for God's wrath.

Their lives are characterized by fear and darkness. By contrast, those who are controlled by the Spirit – who walk according to His ways – have their minds set on what pleases God. They are filled with life and peace. They will still encounter suffering and frustration as they deal with the effects of sin in the world, but the Spirit helps them to endure as they await their final adoption as children of God.

The transformation from being controlled by sin to being controlled by the Spirit is a gift imparted through faith in Christ. When we turn to Jesus and trust Him to save us from our sin, our citizenship is instantly transferred from the kingdom of darkness to the Kingdom of Light. We have a new name, a new identity, and a new future. We are children of light, eagerly awaiting the return of our Savior. And the proof that we belong to Christ is the indwelling, guiding Holy Spirit. We come alive to the Spirit, and He empowers us to put to death the deeds of the flesh.

For if you live according to the flesh you will die, but if by the Spirit you put to death the deeds of the body, you will live. For all who are led by the Spirit of God are sons of God.
ROMANS 8:13-14

As with so many other aspects of the Christian life, there is both an already and a not-yet aspect to the Spirit's work in our lives. In one sense, if we have put our faith in Jesus then we are already controlled by the Spirit. He lives in us and helps us to obey. But in another sense, we still battle our old sin nature every day.

We have to choose life and consciously set our minds on the things of the Spirit. We have to put to death the deeds of the flesh and walk in the deeds of the Spirit. We are heirs of God who cry out to God "Abba, Father," but at the same time we eagerly await our adoption as His children (Rom. 8:15-17, 23).

Moment by moment, we must choose to be controlled by the life-giving Spirit of God.

39

If the Holy Spirit is living in me, why do I still sin?

You've just blown it again. You yelled at the kids, the dog, even your spouse. You said the wrong thing at the wrong time, and you're so angry that you don't even care. If the Holy Spirit is living in you and you're working to keep in step with His commands, why do you still mess up so much? Why must you daily battle against sin?

If you are a Christian, you have died to sin, and now this needs to be taken into account in your daily discipleship. Paul told the Romans, "So you also must consider yourselves dead to sin and alive to God in Christ Jesus" (Rom. 6:11). A few verses later he clarified what this means: "sin will have no dominion over you" (Rom. 6:14).

As Christians, our allegiance has been transferred from one ruler to another. We now belong to God and are free from Satan's grip. Unfortunately, this does not mean that we will not sin. We know this because shortly after proclaiming that we are dead to sin, Paul talks about his own ongoing battle with sin, wherein he continued to do the evil that he did not want to do (Rom. 7:19-20).

So what changed when we aligned ourselves with Christ in His death? We no longer have a settled and irresistible disposition toward sin. The Holy Spirit will convict us when we do what is wrong or fail to do what is right. Sometimes we may fight against His work so that we can continue to enjoy our sin. Other times we will repent of our sin right away and start moving back in the right direction. Either way, we will no longer be comfortable with our sin. The Puritan John Owen said that once we have the Spirit working inside us, our sin becomes a burden that afflicts us rather than a pleasure that delights us.

The other thing that changed when we "died with Christ" is that now we have the power to say no to sin. We will be tempted, but "God is faithful, and he will not let you be tempted beyond your ability, but with the temptation he will also provide the way of escape, that you may be able to endure it" (1 Cor. 10:13). Before we trusted in Jesus, we were powerless over our sin. Now we have Holy Spirit power that enables us to refuse sin and do what is right. By the presence of the Spirit, God Himself helps us not to sin.

I have been crucified with Christ. It is no longer I who live, but Christ who lives in me. And the life I now live in the flesh I live by faith in the Son of God, who loved me and gave himself for me.

GALATIANS 2:20

Nevertheless, even though sin is uncomfortable for us now, and even though God gives us the power to escape its clutches, we still sin. Here, too, the Holy Spirit helps us. He convicts us of sin so that we can repent and return to Jesus. And He keeps us safe in the arms of our Savior, even when we rebel against Him (Rom. 8:15-16). The Holy Spirit guarantees that we are God's children, and assures us that our heavenly Father will never abandon us to our sin.

40

How can I cooperate with the Holy Spirit's work in my life?

We have come a long way in understanding who the Holy Spirit is and what He does. By this point you probably appreciate how important He is in the life of a Christian, so this is a good place to stop and think about what you can do to cooperate with His work in your heart and in your life. This question brings everything we've discussed so far to a point of application, and also prepares us to think about the gifts and fruit of the Spirit in the pages to come.

Because the Holy Spirit's role is to point us to Christ (Jn. 16:14), the pathway to being filled or empowered by the Spirit is through Jesus. So one way to seek the Spirit is indirect – by seeking Jesus. The question isn't just how can I have more of the Holy Spirit, but how can I have more of the Son of God that the Spirit wants to share with me? And the clearest pathway to Jesus is through Holy Scripture, which tells us who Jesus is, why He came, and what He wants us to do.

One of the most basic ways to help the Holy Spirit have more sway over our lives is to read the Bible, meditate on its message, and do what it says. As you focus on and wonder over the glory of Christ, the Spirit will fill you.

Second, we can simply ask for more of the Spirit. Jesus said, "If you then, who are evil, know how to give good gifts to your children, how much more will the heavenly Father give the Holy Spirit to those who ask him!" (Lk. 11:13). Elsewhere Jesus promised that "he gives the Spirit without measure" (Jn. 3:34). There is no limit to how much of the Spirit God wants to give us, and all we have to do to unlock that supernatural blessing is to ask for it. When we pray to receive more of the gift of the Holy Spirit, God will give us abundant, overflowing spiritual life.

Those who live according to the flesh set their minds on the things of the flesh, but those who live according to the Spirit set their minds on the things of the Spirit. For to set the mind on the flesh is death, but to set the mind on the Spirit is life and peace.

ROMANS 8:5-6

A third way we can have more of the Spirit is to make room for Him. When our minds and hearts are cluttered with the cares of this world and our own passions and plans, we don't have much time and energy left over to focus on the things of God. We gradually lose our sense of awe, our ability to hear the Spirit's inward voice, and our desire to honor God. By contrast, when we remove the things that block our view of God – the self-made idols and distractions – we grow in our love for God. Our vision is filled with His glory so that we increasingly desire to obey and serve Him. If you want more of the Holy Spirit's sanctifying power in your life, make Jesus your main priority. Spend your time and resources on things that lift your eyes off of yourself and onto Him. As you do so, the Holy Spirit will blow through your heart with fresh power and peace.

THE GIFTS
OF
the Spirit

41

What are the gifts of the Spirit? Are they the same for every Christian?

We've all heard someone say it, and maybe we've said it ourselves: "I don't really have anything to offer the church." The truth is, every Christian has one or more gifts given by the Holy Spirit to build up the church.

The fact that each believer is given at least one gift (what is called a *charisma* in the original Greek of the New Testament) is emphasized in 1 Corinthians 12:7: "To each is given the manifestation of the Spirit for the common good." These are spiritual gifts, given after salvation by the Holy Spirit. The root of the word charisma is *charis*, which means "grace." So spiritual gifts are supernaturally given graces: they are gifts from God through the Holy Spirit, not mere human talents.

That is not to say that talents are not also gifts of God, or that natural talents cannot be used for the good of the church. But every person on earth is given talents, whereas spiritual gifts only belong to Christians. No matter how new you are to the faith, God the Holy

Spirit has given you a gift that your church needs.

The purpose of spiritual gifts is outlined in Ephesians 4: "Grace was given to each one of us according to the measure of Christ's gift … for building up the body of Christ, until we all attain to the unity of the faith and of the knowledge of the Son of God" (Eph. 4:7, 12-13). Spiritual gifts are not for our own benefit, but for the benefit of the body of Christ. Whatever your particular gifts of the Spirit, they are not yours alone – they belong to the church. And they were not given to you so that you could bring glory to yourself, but so that you could bring glory to God. This is both a privilege, because you do have something important to offer your church, and a responsibility, because you are obligated to share what you have been given to help others mature in the faith.

So what are these gifts of the Spirit? There are five lists given in Scripture (Eph. 4:11; 1 Cor. 12:8-10, 28-30; Rom. 12:6-8; and 1 Pet. 4:11), and there is variety between these lists. Putting the lists together we come up with perhaps nineteen different gifts, and in the coming pages we'll take a closer look at some of the gifts that are mentioned most frequently. The differences between these lists suggest that there is not a fixed or finite list of gifts of the Spirit. Rather, there are workings of the Holy Spirit that fall into general categories of how God uses His people to build up His church.

Rather, speaking the truth in love, we are to grow up in every way into him who is the head, into Christ, from whom the whole body, joined and held together by every joint with which it is equipped, when each part is working properly, makes the body grow so that it builds itself up in love.

EPHESIANS 4:15-16

As you read about different spiritual gifts, ask the Lord to stir in your heart and show you where your gifts lie. Most of all, ask that the Lord will be glorified as you discover and use your gifts for the good of your brothers and sisters in the faith.

42

What is the spiritual gift of tongues?

The gift of tongues is a good place to start thinking about spiritual gifts. This is not because it is the most important gift – in fact it is taught in only one passage – but because it receives the longest treatment and stimulates the most debate. Speaking in tongues is the supernatural ability to speak in a language which the speaker does not know, in earthly languages the hearers know, as at Pentecost (Acts 2:1-4), and some think also perhaps the language of angels (1 Cor. 13:1; 14:2).

There is a vast range of gifts the Spirit gives for building up the church, and each one is valuable (1 Cor. 12:14-31), including tongues. But Paul explicitly warns against elevating the gift of tongues above other gifts, and in fact says that love is more important than any spiritual gift (1 Cor. 13:1). Furthermore, in the list of gifts offered in 1 Corinthians 12:28, the gift of tongues comes last, after prophetic, teaching, healing, and helping gifts.

There are significant challenges inherent in the gift of tongues. Unintelligible speech, even if it comes through the Holy Spirit, is of less benefit than speech that instructs others (1 Cor. 14:1-19). Paul also says that speaking in tongues is speaking not to men but to God, and therefore that it serves to build up the speaker rather than the whole church. For these reasons, the gift of tongues by its very nature requires more safeguards than other spiritual gifts. Speaking in tongues may lead to disorder or emotional manipulation – pitfalls which Paul guards against by insisting on order in the speaking and interpretation of tongues (1 Cor. 14:13-38).

The burning question that arises in almost any discussion of the gift of tongues is whether it was a gift for a particular time in the early church, in which case it is no longer given (this is called the cessationist view), or it is a gift for all times, including today (this is called the charismatic or continuationist view). Different church denominations have answered this question in different ways, and it is well beyond the scope of this book to answer this question.

However, we can say with confidence that studying Paul's words in 1 Corinthians 12 and 14 helps us guard against either dismissing this spiritual gift or over-emphasizing the gift of tongues as a necessary sign of the Holy Spirit's presence. We can also assert that the Holy Spirit is at work today just as He was in the early church. So whether or not the sign of speaking in tongues is the one He chooses to use at a particular time or in a particular place, there are always powerful workings of the Spirit that draw people to faith, just as there were in the early church.

The Holy Spirit is working in our churches and neighborhoods to bring people to Jesus today, and we can join in that task by using our spiritual gifts with joy and exuberance, whether God has given us the gift of tongues or another spiritual gift.

If I speak in the tongues of men and of angels, but have not love, I am a noisy gong or a clanging cymbal.

1 CORINTHIANS 13:1

43

What is the spiritual gift of prophecy?

Both Ephesians 4:11 and 1 Corinthians 12:28-30 list the spiritual gifts of apostleship and prophecy first. We will combine them here because both of these gifts were given through the power of the Holy Spirit while Scripture was being written. Believers did not yet have the benefit of the entire canon of Scripture, so God enabled and empowered certain spokespeople to speak on His behalf.

Prophets spoke messages from God in both the Old and New Testaments. Their words were often prefaced by the phrase "thus says the Lord," lending authority to their words as being straight from God Himself. The apostles were the men commissioned directly by Christ to bear witness to the gospel; all of them were eyewitnesses of the risen Lord Jesus. Their writings make up the bulk of the New Testament, and their preaching formed the basic theology of the Christian church. One of the primary tests of Scripture was whether it was written by a prophet or apostle. God revealed His words, and the prophets and apostles spoke them forth. This was their unique gift for the establishment of the church.

Now that we have the complete Word of God in the Bible, the

gift of prophecy has been replaced by gifts of interpreting Scripture – especially teaching and preaching. God will not speak a new word to us, since Scripture is His completed word to us, but He does gift people with the special ability to interpret or teach what He has said. Their words may be powerful and even in some sense inspired, but they are not new revelations from God. Nor are they infallible. Rather, today's teachers and preachers declare and clarify what God has already spoken through Scripture. God's revelation about Jesus Christ is complete, and now the church's task is to interpret and apply what He has already revealed, not to reveal something new.

The Holy Spirit undeniably gifts some people with a special ability to understand and communicate the truths of Scripture, and some believers seem to possess a special ability to discern God's will about the particulars of their lives. These people may be able to speak a word of truth that helps direct others to a specific decision, one that turns out to be a sovereignly designed choice. These gifts may appear similar to prophetic gifts, and are sometimes called by that name. But we must never confuse them with the prophets of old – those who were the very mouthpiece of God. Every declaration by modern-day "prophets" must be tested against Scripture. These are the words of humans, not of God, and as such are subject to human error. Therefore any decision made with the encouragement of someone's intuition or prophetic-sounding utterances should be undertaken only after testing what they say against Scripture and praying for the Lord's will to be done.

If I have prophetic powers, and understand all mysteries and all knowledge, and if I have all faith, so as to remove mountains, but have not love, I am nothing.

1 CORINTHIANS 13:2

44

What is the spiritual gift of teaching?

Arguably the most important spiritual gift is that of teaching, which is listed in some way in each of the lists of spiritual gifts and is desperately needed in the church today. It is through teaching that people hear God's call to trust in Jesus for salvation (Rom. 10:14). It is through teaching that we obey the final command of Christ to evangelize the world (Mt. 28:19-20). And it is through teaching that the church is built up to the glory of God (Eph. 4:11-12).

The spiritual gift of teaching should not be confused with the natural ability to teach. As with other spiritual gifts, this is a supernatural grace from the Holy Spirit. A nonbeliever may be a talented teacher, but they do not have the spiritual gift of teaching. Likewise a believer may be trained to teach in educational settings but not have the gift of teaching for the church.

Indeed, in some sense every believer should be trained to communicate the truths of Scripture, as teachers do. But those who have the gift of teaching have a special ability to understand and communicate the truths of Scripture. They are able to explain and apply the Word of God in ways that build others up in the faith. The gift of teaching can be developed through training and education, but there is a supernatural component that can neither be taught nor acquired.

What should you do if you believe you may have the gift of teaching? The first thing to do is to try it out. Seek opportunities to teach in your local church, and then get feedback from others. The only way to tell if you have this gift is through the response of those who hear you teach. If you receive a favorable response, work to hone your craft. Study the Bible. Consider attending college or seminary to learn even more. Work at becoming a better communicator by sitting under the teaching of great preachers and teachers.

And he gave the … teachers to equip the saints for the work of ministry, for building up the body of Christ.

EPHESIANS 4:11-12

Though teaching is an important spiritual gift, it should be approached with caution. James issues a sober warning to those who wish to teach: "Not many of you should become teachers, my brothers, for you know that we who teach will be judged with greater strictness" (3:1). Teachers have sway over future generations of Christ followers. If they lead them astray, the entire church will suffer and the name of Christ may even be maligned. For this reason, the gift of teaching is not to be sought for the honor or attention it receives, but rather as a way to humbly serve Christ and His body. Just like any other gift, it should be offered back to God as a sacrifice of thanks for all He has done, for the building up of the body, and not as a means of self-actualization or self-promotion.

45

What is the spiritual gift of mercy or helping?

They are the faithful few who serve week in, week out, with little recognition. They clean the church, make meals for the sick, and help the poor. They buy groceries for the homeless or the home-bound. When something needs to be done, they notice the need, are moved with compassion, and then joyfully step in to get the job done. Simply put, without these people the church could not be the body of Christ, or hands and feet of Christ, to those in need. These are the people with the gift of mercy or helping (1 Cor. 12:28; Rom. 12:7-8).

There are jobs in every church that simply must get done. The two-year-olds need a Sunday school aide. The garbage has to be emptied. Coffee needs to be made and donuts purchased every week for the fellowship hour. Maybe it seems like God doesn't specifically "call" people to these tasks – or perhaps we just close our ears to less desirable callings. And admittedly there are times when each member of the church needs to step up and do the tasks that no one wants to do, simply to serve our brothers and sisters. Everyone in the church can and should help to meet the needs of others.

But there are some people in every church who thrive on opportunities for service. They enjoy stepping in to serve where no one else dares to go. They notice needs that no one else notices, and then quietly step in to meet the need. They don't want or need recognition, they simply love to serve. And while they don't desire notoriety, we should seek opportunities to encourage these saints so that they will not grow weary in doing good (Gal. 6:9). Look around and notice those who seem to always take behind-the-scenes roles to help the church, and then offer a word of thanks or a helping hand. Celebrate their helping gifts of mercy and show them that their service matters.

Having gifts that differ according to the grace given to us, let us use them … the one who does acts of mercy, with cheerfulness.

Romans 12:6, 8

The gift of helping is one of the easiest spiritual gifts to align with natural talents or life circumstances. Are you a good cook? Make meals for people in need. Do you love to hold babies? Sign up for nursery duty. Did you just face a medical crisis? Reach out to someone with a similar diagnosis and offer the help you wish someone had offered you. Are you busy with work or family life? Think of something you already have to do – such as grocery shopping – and find a way to add service to it. Buy an extra bag of food for the food pantry, or call up a friend who has just had surgery and see if she needs you to pick up a few things at the store. Are you already taking care of your own little ones? Think of a single parent who could use a few hours off and offer to babysit. The opportunities to use the gifts of mercy and helping are limited only by your creativity and your willingness to serve.

46

What is the spiritual gift of administration?

Imagine a church led only by visionaries who seem to sense God's will but have no ability to organize themselves or others to carry it out. Nothing would ever get done. On the other hand, if all we have is administrators and organizers with no creative dreams for the future, we will only do what seems pragmatic and may miss out on seeing God powerfully work in our congregations. We need all the spiritual gifts, working together, to accomplish God's purposes for the church in the world – including the gift of leadership (Rom. 12:8) or administration (1 Cor. 12:28). Christians are sometimes tempted to diminish these gifts as "unspiritual" because they are practical gifts that often make use of worldly wisdom. But these gifts, too, are given by the Holy Spirit.

Administrators and leaders are those who see the best path forward for doing the work at hand. They can tell what jobs need to be done and identify the best person for each job. They readily grasp the best practices for managing people and resources and are able to guide the church to wisely steward what God has given to effectively expand Christ's Kingdom.

The most important characteristic that must accompany the gift of administration in order for it to be used effectively is humility. A humble leader is one who understands that their abilities and authority come from God and are given for the good of the Kingdom of God. They use their position not to boss people around, but to help them grow and to give them opportunities to serve. In addition, leaders must be spiritually mature so that they can rightly discern God's will for the future. And they must have the ability to communicate winsomely and persuasively so they can guide others into right decisions based on the Word of God. They are called to stand up courageously for what is right and remain unswayed by popular opinion.

Leadership is often a lonely gift. Others may not like the decisions you have to make, or they may feel slighted if you give responsibilities they wanted to

If one member suffers, all suffer together; if one member is honored, all rejoice together.

1 CORINTHIANS 12:26

someone who may or may not be more qualified to carry them out. For this reason, people who have the gift of administration should maintain close relationships with friends who can encourage them during dark times and hold them accountable to keep their relationship with God vibrant. Because of your leadership or administrative position, you should find friends and confidants among other leaders, including those outside your congregation.

If you are a support person for someone with the gift of leadership, take your role seriously. Think of ways to help your leaders rest so they don't burn out. Keep the lines of communication open so they can turn to you in times of need. Most importantly, pray for them regularly – that they will abide in Christ, that they will be able to withstand temptation, and that God will give them wisdom to lead well.

47

What is the spiritual gift of discernment?

Discernment is the ability to distinguish between right and wrong, or between truth and error, particularly in situations when it may be difficult to do so. This is an ability that every believer develops to some extent as they mature in the faith. Hebrews 5:13-14 says, "Everyone who lives on milk is unskilled in the word of righteousness, since he is a child. But solid food is for the mature, for those who have their powers of discernment trained by constant practice to distinguish good from evil." The more we steep ourselves in the truths of Scripture, the better we are able to distinguish good from evil.

Some Christians also have what Paul calls "the ability to distinguish between spirits" (1 Cor. 12:10). This type of discernment goes beyond the judgment that every believer gains as they grow in the faith; this is a gift from the Holy Spirit. It is a supernatural ability to see what is going on beneath the surface.

The gift of distinguishing spirits enables people to see through the deceit of false teachers and false doctrines. Satan's *modus operandi* since the Garden of Eden has been to twist the truth subtly, so we can't tell exactly where the lie is, and thus we are drawn into his deception.

Many will be fooled by the schemes of Satan and by wolves in sheep's clothing, but those with the gift of distinguishing spirits will be able to tell truth from error and rebuke those who would harm God's people. They are able to tell whether things that look like gifts of the Holy Spirit are mere human imitations, deceptions of Satan, or the real thing.

As with so many other spiritual gifts, the discipline of discerning or "testing the spirits" (1 Jn. 4:1) is something every believer is called to do. Like the Bereans of old, we are to "[receive] the word with all eagerness, examining the Scriptures daily to see if these things [are] so" (Acts 17:11). Whether or not you have the spiritual gift of distinguishing the spirits, you can and should seek to grow in discernment.

By this you know the Spirit of God: every spirit that confesses that Jesus Christ has come in the flesh is from God, and every spirit that does not confess Jesus is not from God.
1 JOHN 4:2-3

Study the Bible daily so that you can distinguish truth from error, and glean insights from those who are more mature and wise in the faith. Then thank the Holy Spirit for gracing the church with gifted people who guide us when it is hard for us to know what is right.

48

What is the spiritual gift of generosity?

We have all met someone who would literally "give the shirt off his back" to help us. Perhaps we complimented an item they owned and they turned around and gave it to us without a second thought. Or maybe we received an anonymous gift card or a check during a financial crisis. If so, we've been blessed by the gift of generosity. People who have this gift like to share it; they delight in giving away what God has given them.

The spiritual gift of generosity has as its foundation the realization that everything we have comes from God. Because He is Creator and Almighty God, we are merely stewards of what He rightfully owns – and could at any moment take away from us. Furthermore, everything in this life is of minimal value when compared with the surpassing riches of eternal life with God. This realization causes us to hold our possessions more loosely. If we don't own it and can't take it with us when we die, we might as well use it to further God's eternal purposes.

Some Christians with the gift of generosity are blessed with greater material blessings than their neighbors. Paul says, "He who supplies seed to the sower and bread for food will supply and multiply your seed for sowing" (2 Cor. 9:10), a concept that is echoed throughout the Bible. As we give our resources for spreading the gospel, thus proving that our hearts and our pocketbooks belong to God, He may bless us with more so that we can give more. When we are generous with what we have, God often entrusts us with even more resources.

Of course, not every person who has the gift of generosity is rich by the world's standards. Some Christians have very little, but they love to give what they have. Jesus held up the woman who gave only two copper coins as an example of generosity (Mk. 12:41-44). Generosity has more to do with the size of the giver's heart than the size of their gift. In addition, we are called to give more than our money. We can also be generous with our time, our abilities, or our hospitality. Whenever someone consistently gives abundantly of whatever God has given to them, they are exercising the spiritual gift of generosity.

So we, though many, are one body in Christ, and individually members one of another. Having gifts that differ according to the grace given to us, let us use them: ... the one who contributes, in generosity.

ROMANS 12:5-6, 8

Whether we have the spiritual gift of generosity or not, every Christian is called to give generously. Since "every good gift and every perfect gift is from above, coming down from the Father of lights" (James 1:17), whenever and whatever we give, we are merely returning to God what is rightfully His. Everything we have comes from His hand, and offering it back to Him as an act of worship is the appropriate response to His generous grace. Furthermore, our example is God Himself, who has generously given to us the greatest gift of all – our Lord Jesus, who "though he was rich, yet for your sake he became poor, so that you by his poverty might become rich" (2 Cor. 8:9).

117

49

What is the spiritual gift of evangelism?

Every Christian is given the task of evangelizing or sharing the good news. This is the Great Commission that Jesus gave us: to go into all the world with the gospel (Mt. 28:18-20). We are "ambassadors for Christ, God making his appeal through us" (2 Cor. 5:20). But there are some people who seem to have a special knack for sharing their faith – what we know as the spiritual gift of evangelism. These people are able to communicate winsomely the message that Christ died for sinners, seemingly with anyone and everyone they meet. They are able to strike up a conversation about spiritual things when many people don't see an opening. Their message is clear and concise, and frequently the people they share with respond to the love of God.

It is useful to note what the gift of evangelism is not. Evangelism is not someone telling others about Jesus because they feel duty-bound to do so. Guilt is not the motivation here. Like the other spiritual gifts, evangelism is a grace from the Holy Spirit, and for those who have the gift, sharing is a joy. They can't stop talking about God because they are so excited about what He has done for them.

The gift of evangelism is not limited to a particular personality type. This gift is not only given to extroverts, the kind of people who "never meet a stranger." Nor is it only for people in a certain profession. Billy Graham certainly had the gift of evangelism, but so does the cashier at McDonald's who shares the love of Jesus with her coworkers, or the bank manager who has a weekly Bible study in his office. There are evangelists in every occupation, all around the world.

Perhaps the most important thing for us to note about the gift of evangelism is that Christians cannot let themselves off the hook by saying "it's not my gift" and leaving the good work of sharing the gospel completely to others. Every Christian is called to share the love of Jesus. We may not think we are particularly good at it, but we are still responsible for the Great Commission: "Go therefore and make disciples of all nations" (Mt. 28:19). If we love God we will want others to love Him too, and if we love our neighbors we will want to help them receive the same great salvation that we have found.

> *As for you, always be sober-minded, endure suffering, do the work of an evangelist, fulfill your ministry.*
> 2 TIMOTHY 4:5

God has given you particular experiences and a unique sphere of influence, and He wants you to use your abilities and your circumstances to reach the people He has placed in your path. The most important question isn't "do I have the gift of evangelism?" but rather "am I loving God and loving my neighbor by sharing the good news of the gospel where God has placed me?" Or perhaps more to the point, "Am I making the most of every opportunity to evangelize?" (Col. 4:5), as every Christian should.

50

What is the spiritual gift of healing?

When Jesus walked the earth, He did so as the healer of both body and soul. On one occasion Jesus healed a paralyzed man by forgiving his sins (Mk. 2:5), and when the Pharisees criticized Him for doing this, Jesus said, "Those who are well have no need of a physician, but those who are sick. I came not to call the righteous, but sinners" (Mk. 2:17). Jesus had tender compassion for those who suffered in the body, but His primary concern was the state of their soul.

The tandem concerns of physical and spiritual well-being live on in the ministry of the church today. We long for people to be healed from physical as well as spiritual sickness. When we or someone we love comes down with a serious illness or has a life-changing accident, we wonder about the possibility of healing. What is the spiritual gift of healing, and how can we tell if someone has it?

When the Bible talks about the spiritual gift of healing, it is closely linked with miracles (1 Cor. 12:9-10, 28). In other words, this is not merely healing through the use of physical or medicinal means to effect a cure – the reference in this passage is to supernatural healing. This brings up the question of whether the gift of healing, like the gifts of tongues and prophecy, is still in existence today, or whether it was a gift given for a particular time during the establishment of the church. The placement of the gift of healing between other gifts that definitely continue today – wisdom, knowledge, faith, and discerning of spirits in verses 8-10 and teaching and healing in verses 28-30 – suggests that the gift of healing also continues today. In addition, there are accounts of healings and miracles throughout church history and also in many places around the world today.

There are many counterfeits to the gift of healing. Some people fake the gift of healing through clever camera tricks or playacting to gain an audience or amass a fortune. So how can we tell whether a healing is from God? As with other spiritual gifts, we can discern truth from error by the fruit. Those with the spiritual gift of healing will use it to advance the Kingdom of God, not their own kingdoms. They will give the glory to God and acknowl-

> *To each is given the manifestation of the Spirit for the common good. ... to another gifts of healing by the one Spirit, to another the working of miracles. ... All these are empowered by one and the same Spirit, who apportions to each one individually as he wills.*
>
> 1 CORINTHIANS 12:7, 9-11

edge that He is the healer, and they are merely the conduits of His grace. And, of course, the healing will be true and lasting healing.

We are right to long and pray for ourselves and for those we love to be healed. Sickness is part of the fall, not how the world was created to be. God has promised total healing, but not in this life – only in the life to come. In the meantime, we must keep in mind that our true need is for Jesus – for Him to touch our souls and heal us from sin, to flood us with peace and love, and to make us His dear children, which is what we need both in this life and the life to come.

51

What does the Bible mean by "fruit of the Spirit"?

The name should tip us off to the difference between *gifts* of the Spirit and *fruit* of the Spirit: gifts are given differently to each believer, just as we would not give the same gift to everyone on our list at Christmastime. But fruit is something every believer should produce. It is the natural result of remaining in Christ (Jn. 15). To put it another way, the same Spirit who gives a variety of gifts (1 Cor. 12:4) grows every believer to be more and more like Jesus (2 Cor. 3:18).

The fruit of the Spirit is listed in Galatians 5:22-23: "The fruit of the Spirit is love, joy, peace, patience, kindness, goodness, faithfulness, gentleness, self-control; against such things there is no law." These verses come just after a discussion on walking in the Spirit and living in freedom. Although at first the idea of walking in obedience and being free from the law may seem paradoxical, the Bible sees no contradiction between our ongoing, conscious effort to live a godly life – putting to death the deeds of the flesh (Rom.

8:13; Col. 3:5) – and the fact that the power to grow in grace comes from God through the Holy Spirit (Gal. 3:3). Sanctification is not *either* a work of human effort *or* a work of the Holy Spirit, it is both. And growing the fruit of the Spirit is part of our sanctification. Galatians gives us a list of the characteristics of God Himself that we will exhibit in greater and greater amounts as we grow closer to Him.

Just like natural fruit is produced by a growth process, so it is with fruit of the Spirit. We will not produce these things overnight, but as we gradually grow in the knowledge of Christ, we will begin to produce these spiritual graces in ever-increasing quantities. When we draw life from Christ, growing deep roots by feeding on the Bible, we will become stronger in faith and then will supernaturally produce fruit that reflects the life-giver Himself. Over time, more growth will lead to more fruit.

The fruit of the Spirit is love, joy, peace, patience, kindness, goodness, faithfulness, gentleness, self control; against such things there is no law.

GALATIANS 5.22-23

Taking the analogy one step further, just as fruit does not exist for the good of the tree, the fruit that the Spirit produces is not for us. The characteristics listed in Galatians 5:22-23 are designed to benefit others. When we grow in love, joy, peace, and all the rest, we will become people who are more pleasant to be around. And more than that, we will become people who give life to others. The Spirit's work in us will give those around us a taste of what God is like. And after just one taste they will want more – more of the God who is perfectly loving, joyful, peace-giving, and patient. Then the fruit that the Holy Spirit is growing in us will also be produced in them.

52

What is the
spiritual fruit of love?

Jesus said that love is the sum of all the other commandments: "You shall love the Lord your God with all your heart and with all your soul and with all your mind. This is the great and first commandment. And a second is like it: You shall love your neighbor as yourself. On these two commandments depend all the Law and the Prophets" (Mt. 22:37-40). If we learn to love God and our neighbor as we ought, we will obey all the other commandments as well. But if we don't have love, all of our other work for the Lord is as abrasive and pointless as a noisy gong or clanging cymbal (1 Cor. 13:1-3). Without love, we are nothing.

The Bible shows through both example and command what this all-important love looks like. Love is all the attributes we read about in 1 Corinthians 13 – patience, kindness, gentleness, and the rest. It is caring for those who cannot repay – the poor, the orphans, and the widows. Love is being kind and fair in our business dealings and in our personal relationships. It is acting toward others with a humility and selflessness that communicates their worth as people made in God's image. The ultimate example of love, of course, is Jesus sacrificing His life for us, giving up everything for people who were His enemies. In short, love is treating others in the way we would like to be treated but don't deserve.

In His teaching about love, Jesus calls out lawkeepers who pervert the laws of love to make them easier to obey (Mt. 5:21-48). Such people think they are doing fine at loving others if they avoid the big, public sins like murder or adultery. But Jesus says that even a careless remark or a lustful thought breaks the rule of love. Nor is it enough to love people for whom we feel affection. Like the Pharisees, we want to limit our neighbors to people who are like us, or who at least are likeable. But Jesus taught us that our neighbor is anyone we come in contact with, even our enemy (Mt. 5:43-45).

God's love has been poured into our hearts through the Holy Spirit who has been given to us.

ROMANS 5:5

Perhaps you wonder sometimes how you can ever love as you ought. The truth is, we are unloving and unlovely people, and keeping the command to love may be the hardest thing we will ever do. Love is more than simply avoiding hatred; it is doing good to others even when they don't deserve it. So it is good news that love is a fruit of the Holy Spirit. The God of the universe, who loved us so much that He died to save us, can empower us to love our neighbors as ourselves. He pours His love into our hearts and makes our love grow, guiding and empowering us as we seek to obey God's command to love.

53

What is the spiritual fruit of joy?

Christians should be the most joyful people on earth, for we know that our sins are forgiven and one day we will worship God face-to-face in heaven for all eternity. Joy – and its companion, hope – should characterize our lives. In Biblical terms, joy is the proper response to God's saving work of grace and all the blessings He gives us. It is the result of believing in the good that God has done and has promised to do.

Of course there will be times when we sorrow. Even Jesus wept over the death of a friend (Jn. 11:35) and was anguished over His own impending death (Mk. 14:33). Jesus was repeatedly moved with compassion for the crowds He ministered to. He entered into our sorrowful situation, and so He is able to empathize with us and bring comfort through the ministry of the Holy Spirit.

We should feel sorrow over sin and its effects, and for the brokenness we see around us. This world is not as it should be, for we were created for a perfect world as God originally made it. At times we may even sink into despair over the suffering we experience in our own lives and witness in the lives of people we love. But we must never grieve as those without hope (1 Thess. 4:13). We must not let our sorrow over sin drift into self-indulgent depression or self-pity. It's a question of motives: worldly sorrow comes from a frustrated ego or unbelief, whereas godly sorrow is repentant and full of faith.

How can we keep our joy in the Holy Spirit? The key is not to place our hope and joy in ourselves, our circumstances, or the world around us. The root of joy is faith that God is who He says He is and will do what He has promised. God made us and delights in us. He forgives our sins and is preparing a new home in heaven for us, where there will be no more sorrow or dying or pain. He daily lavishes His love and favor on us. He is all-wise and all-knowing, and therefore the sorrows we face have a purpose. They also have an end date. If we truly believe these things, we cannot help but be joyful.

May the God of hope fill you with all joy and peace in believing, so that by the power of the Holy Spirit you may abound in hope.

Romans 15:13

God has given us many things for our enjoyment, and it is right that we find deep joy in time spent with loved ones or the satisfaction of a job well done. Our delight in God's good is an act of worship when we acknowledge Him as the giver. But we must keep these joys in perspective. Even the best joys in life are temporary, fleeting pleasures. True, lasting joy is found in God alone. As we spend time in His Word, meditating on all He has done for us and all His promises that are yet to be fulfilled, we will find deep, abiding joy that lasts through good times and bad. Our joy in God's blessings will increase, and so will the hope that anchors our soul in times of sorrow.

54

What is the spiritual fruit of peace?

In our hurried and harried existence, perhaps the most fleeting fruit of the Spirit is peace. We long for peace, for *shalom*, for a settled life free from anxiety and strife. We know that Jesus is the Prince of Peace, but this doesn't seem to have much bearing on our daily lives. Often we feel like the disciples in the storm, crying out to Jesus, "Do you not care that we are perishing?" (Mk. 4:38). How can we have peace when our lives seem to be spinning out of control?

Like the fruit of joy, true peace comes from God Himself, not from anything the world can give us. In the Old Testament God established a covenant of peace with His people using these words: "'The mountains may depart and the hills be removed, but my steadfast love shall not depart from you, and my covenant of peace shall not be removed,' says the LORD, who has compassion on you" (Isa. 54:10). God has promised to give His people peace, but He has not promised an easy life. Peace as God defines it is unrelated to the ease or unease of our earthly existence.

The Christian's peace has as its foundation the fact that we are reconciled to God through Jesus' death and resurrection: "Therefore, since we have been justified by faith, we have peace with God through our Lord Jesus Christ. Through him we have also obtained access by faith into this grace in which we stand" (Rom. 5:1-2). It is a settled fact that if we believe in Jesus for salvation, we have peace with God. We who were once God's enemies have been made His friends. More than that, we have been adopted as His children. As we embrace our position as God's beloved child, we will be able to live at peace with others as well, extending to them the grace that we have received from God.

The peace God gives is more than the absence of enmity. It is His peace that crushes Satan (Rom. 16:20), sanctifies us (1 Thess. 5:23), and brings life (Heb. 13:20). It is not passive, it is active. The process for growing this spiritual fruit in our lives is active as well. As we consciously and continually realign ourselves with God's promises, trusting that He loves us and will do good for us, we can have peace that surpasses understanding (Phil. 4:7). We can rest free from anxiety because we know that no matter what the future holds, God is holding us in His strong hands.

We don't need to worry about our financial troubles, family trials, fears about the future, or anything else because nothing can happen to us outside His will, and His will for us is our eternal good. Peace is knowing that we are in the boat with Jesus, and at just the right time He will tell the storm, "Peace! Be still!" and it will be calm (Mk. 4:39).

Let the peace of Christ rule in your hearts, to which indeed you were called in one body. And be thankful.

COLOSSIANS 3:15

55

What is the spiritual fruit of patience?

There are plenty of things to be impatient about. Our life isn't progressing on the timetable we had hoped. The person in front of us in line can't seem to make up their mind about what to order. Our toddler is disobeying again. And again. About the same thing. Or perhaps even worse, we can't seem to keep ourselves from making the same mistake over and over. In short, we have an idea of how things ought to go and when they ought to happen, and life isn't meeting our expectations. The root of our impatience is pride – the belief that we know better than someone else, that our time is more precious than theirs, or worst of all, that we know better than God Himself.

Patience is a virtue that is interconnected with other virtues. On the one hand, we will grow in patience as we grow in faith and hope. The more we trust that God knows best and has our ultimate good in mind, the more patient we will be with His work in our lives. As our faith grows, so will our patience. Likewise, if we have hope in God's promise of heaven, we will be able to endure more patiently the suffering we face in this life. We will understand how fleeting our momentary troubles are when compared with the eternal glories of heaven, and we will allow suffering to have its way so we can develop perseverance (Rom. 5:3).

There is also a close correlation between patience and the other fruit of the Spirit. As we grow in patience we will find it easier to be loving, kind, and gentle with others when we are under stress. In fact, elsewhere the apostle Paul lists patience as the first characteristic of love (1 Cor. 13:4). The Greek word for *patience* both in 1 Corinthians 13 and in the list of the fruit of the Spirit in Galatians 5 literally means "long temper" or "long suffering." Those who have the spiritual fruit of patience bear with the faults and foibles of others. They take the time to understand why someone is acting as they are, and then they lovingly bear with the growth process. They don't allow minor annoyances to ruffle them, because they have a long-term perspective on life and eternity.

As with every other fruit of the Spirit, the source and model of patience is the Triune God, who is slow to anger and abounding in steadfast love (Ps. 103:8). God "endures with much patience" our sinful ways (Rom. 9:22). Jesus lived this out in His relationship with His disciples, who often failed Him. Now the Holy Spirit exercises the same kind of patience with us. We are every bit as sinful as the people we get impatient with, and yet the perfect God bears with us in love. How can we not extend that same long-suffering patience to our brothers and sisters? Who are we to express impatience toward others, when God has patiently borne with us?

> *Walk in a manner worthy of the calling to which you have been called, with all humility and gentleness, with patience, bearing with one another in love, eager to maintain the unity of the Spirit in the bond of peace.*
>
> EPHESIANS 4:1-3

56

What is the spiritual fruit of kindness?

At first glance, kindness can seem like a somewhat benign attribute. We use it as a synonym for "nice," and remind our children to be kind as if we are simply reminding them to say please and thank you. We think of kindness as the opposite of being mean, as if we can be polite but indifferent and still call it kindness. But the Biblical definition of kindness is so much more.

The Greek word for *kindness* is related to words for "useful," "serviceable," and "effective." It is an active word that connotes thoughtfully seeking to benefit another person. Kindness is the inner disposition, born in us by the Holy Spirit, that makes us compassionate toward the needs of others and moved to take action to meet those needs. It is the loving motivation to do good to someone, even if it costs us something. Kindness involves sensitivity and sacrifice. A closely related attribute is humility, for when we think of others as more important than ourselves, we will act kindly toward them. Thus kindness is one antidote to selfishness and pride.

The ultimate example of kindness is God. Kindness is the attribute of God that especially draws us to repentance

(Rom. 2:4). It is the part of His nature that offers us salvation (Tit. 3:4-5). Indeed, Jesus Himself is the greatest expression of the kindness of God, for when He saw what we needed, He came to dwell among us and die for us (Eph. 2:7). We have been saved through the loving kindness of God, and knowing this should move us to extend kindness to others.

Put on then, as God's chosen ones, holy and beloved, compassionate hearts, kindness, humility, meekness, and patience.

COLOSSIANS 3:12

Jesus gave us a notable example of kindness in the Parable of the Good Samaritan (Lk. 10:25-37). In this story a Jewish man was robbed, beaten, and left for dead. A priest and a Levite – clergymen who should have understood the character of God well enough to offer kindness to a person in need, walked by in self-righteous pride. They did not have the spiritual fruit of kindness. By contrast, the Samaritan – a member of a race despised by the Jews as worthless – saw the man's need and responded with kindness. The person we would least expect to be kind in this story was the only one who showed kindness, setting an example for all of us.

In telling this story, Jesus was illustrating whom we should be kind to – not just our friends, but anyone in need, even our enemies. He was also showing who has the ability to be kind – anyone who receives the grace of God. As the story points out, kindness involves personal sacrifice. It is reaching out to someone who doesn't deserve our kindness and going out of our way to help. May we who understand the kindness of God realize how undeserving we are of His kindness, and respond by reaching out to others with kind, sacrificial deeds.

57

What is the spiritual fruit of goodness?

The word *good* has become cheapened in our vocabulary. "He's such a good boy," we say, meaning little more than that he is relatively quiet and stays out of serious trouble. We think of good in contrast to bad, and if something is not *too* bad then it must be good. But in Biblical terms, goodness means so much more.

Goodness is the essence of God's nature, an aspect of who He *is*. He doesn't just *do* good, He *is* good. Because of this, God cannot do anything other than good (Rom. 8:28). A children's song reminds us of this truth: "God is so good, He's so good to me." God's goodness is something that we can taste and see (Ps. 34:8). And it is for all people, not just believers: "The LORD is good to all, and his mercy is over all that he has made" (Ps. 145:9).

The spiritual fruit of goodness is first of all moral purity. It is the opposite of evil. It is the deliberate choosing of right over wrong, striving for holiness in all things. Believers exhibit the fruit of goodness when they filter their entertainment choices, favoring things that are morally excellent and rejecting things that are vulgar or disreputable. Goodness is noticing and abhorring the evil in the world, and seeking to remain unstained by it. The apostle Paul gave us a picture of what goodness looks like when he wrote, "Whatever is true, whatever is honorable, whatever is just, whatever is pure, whatever is lovely, whatever is commendable, if there is any excellence, if there is anything worthy of praise" (Phil. 4:8). These are the good things we should think about, and when we do so we will exhibit the spiritual fruit of goodness.

Goodness is also an action – the exercise of compassion. It is showing God's goodness through word and deed. Believers with the fruit of goodness, though they are bothered by lifestyles that are in opposition to God's commands, will still be kind to those who live that way. They will seek to help and benefit others, particularly those in need. They will think of others before themselves and act in a kind and compassionate way. Goodness is putting action to our faith, providing food and clothing for our brothers and sisters (James 2:14-26).

> *So then, as we have opportunity, let us do good to everyone, and especially to those who are of the household of faith.*
> GALATIANS 6:10

As we reclaim the deep beauty of goodness, understanding the moral purity and faithful action involved, we will better understand the goodness of God toward us. God is good, all the time. Even when we suffer, God is still good. He is perfect in all His judgments and kind in the way He cares for us. Every moment He is showing us mercy and kindness, if we have eyes to see it, and He is perfecting us through our trials so that we can be good through and through – not just good on the outside, but truly good.

58

What is the spiritual fruit of faithfulness?

Even the most ardent atheist, a person who prides himself on lack of faith, values faithfulness. We admire faithfulness in marriage and honor faithfulness to a cause or career. But while human beings may achieve a measure of faithfulness in one area or another, we can't understand perfect faithfulness apart from God. He is the only one who is absolutely, unchangingly, and eternally faithful.

Synonyms for faithfulness include trustworthiness, constancy, loyalty, and steadfastness. Faithfulness is following through on commitments and keeping promises, regardless of emotions or moods that might tempt us to do otherwise. In the Biblical sense, faithfulness is believing what God says and acting on that belief. It is aligning ourselves with truth and continuing on the path of living out our faith. It is a settled pattern of behavior that is consistent with what we profess. By contrast, unfaithfulness is being undependable. It is saying one thing and doing another. In the end, unfaithfulness is disobedience and rebellion against God, who always does what He says.

It is possible to appear to be faithful, yet not truly be so. Such inconsistency often leads to legalism, where people go through the motions of obedience or devotion to God, but are only doing it for show. They do not truly give God their best, they only give what costs them nothing. This is hypocrisy and half-heartedness. What God desires from us is true devotion, from the heart, so He despises all unfaithfulness.

Our supreme and perfect example in faithfulness is God. The psalmist writes, "Forever, O LORD, your word is firmly fixed in the heavens. Your faithfulness endures to all generations; you have established the earth, and it stands fast" (Ps. 119:89-90). God's faithfulness is based on His unchanging nature. He is eternally the same, absolutely perfect in all His ways. For this reason, we can trust in Him absolutely, with no shadow of doubt. We never have to wonder if He will change His mind about us, or take away our salvation. What He has promised, He will do. This includes the example of Jesus, who was faithful unto death

No unbelief made him waver concerning the promise of God, but he grew strong in his faith as he gave glory to God, fully convinced that God was able to do what he had promised.

ROMANS 4:20-21

(Phil. 2:8) and challenges us to do the same (Rev. 2:10).

The faithfulness of God is where our power to be faithful comes from. We can be faithful because the Holy Spirit enables us to keep our commitments, and because the Spirit is utterly faithful, He will keep on enabling us to be faithful too. Our part is to continue in the path of obedience. As we determine in our hearts to obey God, and set ourselves to that task, the Holy Spirit will give us the strength to follow through. As we remind ourselves of God's holiness, our awe of Him helps drive us to faithful obedience. When we pattern ourselves after the God who does not change, purposing to be true to our word and constant in our duty, this is the path of faithfulness as the Spirit intends.

59

What is the spiritual fruit of gentleness?

An old hymn describes "gentle Jesus, meek and mild." We may argue about whether this is an adequate description for the Savior who cast out demons, rebuked religious leaders in public, and overturned the tables of the moneychangers in the Temple, but these lyrics properly relate the interconnected concepts of gentleness and meekness.

One common definition for gentleness (or meekness) is "strength under control." It is not weakness or feebleness. Rather, it is restraint motivated by humility. Humanly speaking, the right assessment of God's greatness and our unworthiness moves us to reverent behavior. Far from being a sign of weakness, gentleness is a fruit of the Spirit that requires great strength.

The fruit of gentleness can be understood by looking at its opposites and counterfeits. The opposite of gentleness is unrestrained anger and revenge – making rash judgments and imposing them on others. By contrast, gentleness includes resting in the judgments of God and leaving vengeance to Him. This reveals the connection between humility and gentleness. The counterfeit of gentleness is false modesty and simpering spinelessness. People who refuse to stand up for what is right are not gentle, they are cowards. That is why gentleness requires strength and courage.

Gentleness was modeled by Jesus in His triumphal entry, where we read, "Behold, your king is coming to you, humble, and mounted on a donkey, on a colt, the foal of a beast of burden" (Mt. 21:5). The word translated as "humble" is often translated as "meek" or "gentle," and it is the same root word as gentleness in Galatians 5:23. Jesus rightly deserved the horses and chariots of heaven and the total devotion of all people, but instead He humbled Himself to ride a donkey on His way to die for the sins of people who did not love Him. Jesus shows us meekness or gentleness in all its beauty.

Remind them to be submissive to rulers and authorities, to be obedient, to be ready for every good work, to speak evil of no one, to avoid quarreling, to be gentle, and to show perfect courtesy toward all people.

TITUS 3:1-2

The attributes that we typically associate with gentleness – things like quiet kindness and soft tenderness – are outgrowths of the true character of gentleness. When we properly understand God's place as the sovereign, all-wise, all-powerful Creator, we naturally leave the judgments to Him. We rightly assess our own unworthiness of God's love and put the needs of others before ourselves because we value them as God does. Rather than bending things to our will or lashing out in anger when things do not go our way, we set aside control and restrain our rash emotions. Gentleness all comes back to a humble realization of our place in the world as an imperfect, rebellious creature who nevertheless is deeply loved by the Creator.

60

What is the spiritual fruit of self-control?

There is a good reason Paul ends his list of the fruit of the Spirit with self-control. This is the virtue that helps us live out all the others. We may want to be loving, joyful, at peace, and so forth – but if we have not learned to keep our selfish desires under control, we will not be loving or joyful or at peace. Left to our own devices, we tend toward sin, selfishness, and self-indulgence. But with the Holy Spirit's help, we can learn to reign in our sinful desires so that we can walk in godliness.

Unlike the other fruit of the Spirit, self-control is not a characteristic of God the Father. Because God is perfect, he doesn't need to control sinful desires. But Jesus, when He walked the earth as a man, was subject to the same kinds of trials and temptations that we face (Heb. 4:15). He had to choose to obey the Father's will even when He didn't want to. When He was on trial, Jesus did not open His mouth (1 Pet. 2:23). Though He was God and thus could do anything He wanted, Jesus chose the suffering of the cross for us. He is the perfect example of self-control.

The old-fashioned word for self-control is temperance. It the rejection of desires that are not good for us, or are not the greater good. Examples include things like controlling our temper and limiting our intake of food to a healthy amount. Keeping to God's boundaries for sex – as a gift to be enjoyed only within the bond of a marriage between a man and a woman – also requires self-control. Opposites of self-control include some of the so-called "deadly sins": greed, gluttony, lust, wrath, and sloth. But self-control means more than just refusing to give in to sinful desires; it is also disciplining ourselves to do what is right. It is choosing to help someone else rather than spend our time and money on desirable pleasures. It is choosing wholesome entertainment or a healthy meal. It is disciplining our bodies and minds for godliness.

For the grace of God has appeared, bringing salvation for all people, training us to renounce ungodliness and worldly passions, and to live self-controlled, upright, and godly lives in the present age.

TITUS 2:11-12

The attribute of self-discipline is a large part of self-control, and we can learn self-discipline through practices that are sometimes called spiritual disciplines. These practices, when done regularly, will help us abide in Christ and reign in our selfish impulses. The list of spiritual disciplines varies, but usually includes Bible reading, prayer, memorizing and meditating on Scripture, acts of service, and fasting. These are things we should do on a regular basis to aid in our spiritual growth. They are not spiritual fruit themselves, but the Spirit uses them to grow us in the likeness of Christ. As Paul told his protégé Timothy: "Train yourself for godliness; for while bodily training is of some value, godliness is of value in every way, as it holds promise for the present life and also for the life to come" (1 Tim. 4:7-8). We must prioritize self-control lest we become controlled by self.

Nancy Taylor

has spent the past 17 years
raising her brood of five children
while maintaining an active freelance
writing and editing schedule. Born
and raised in Wheaton, Illinois,
she is a graduate of Wheaton College
with a degree in English and
Christian Education.

Philip Ryken

is President of Wheaton College.
A graduate of Wheaton College,
Westminster Theological Seminary,
and the University of Oxford,
Dr. Ryken is the author of more than
forty Bible commentaries and
other books on Christianity and culture.
He also serves as a board member for
the Lausanne Movement and the
National Association of Evangelicals.

Notes